# BOLOUGNE-SUR-MER

# BOLOUGNE-SUR-MER

## WILLIAM CANON FLEMING

ISBN: 978-93-5420-827-0

Published:                1907

LECTOR HOUSE LLP
E-MAIL: lectorpublishing@gmail.com

**BOULOGNE-SUR-MER**

The cross marks the ruins of the fortifications built around Caligula's
Tower by Henry VIII., King of England.

# BOULOGNE-SUR-MER

## ST. PATRICK'S NATIVE TOWN

BY

### THE REV. WILLIAM CANON FLEMING,

RECTOR OF ST. MARY'S, MOORFIELDS, LONDON

1907

Nihil Obstat.

GULIRLMUS CANONICUS GILDEA, D.D., M.R.

Imprimatur.

✠ FRANCISCUS,

*Archiepiscopus Westmonasteriensis.*

THIS HISTORY OF ST. PATRICK'S NATIVE TOWN
IS AFFECTIONATELY DEDICATED TO THE
RIGHT REVEREND PATRICK FENTON,
BISHOP OF AMYCLA
AND
BISHOP AUXILIARY OF WESTMINSTER.

# PREFACE.

THE numerous bewildering and contradictory theories to be met with in books, pamphlets, and reviews concerning St. Patrick's native country are calculated to provoke a spirit of weary incredulity and impatience. However, when presenting this book to the public, we may quote the late Canon O'Hanlon's plea for adventurous writers who still endeavour to solve the problem: "The question of St. Patrick's country," writes the distinguished author of the "Lives of the Irish Saints," " has an interest for all candid investigators far beyond the claim of rival nations for the honour it should confer. It has been debated, indeed, with considerable learning and earnestness both by Irish and foreign writers; yet, as Ireland does not prefer any serious claim to the distinction, of which she might well feel proud, so can Irishmen afford to be impartial in prosecuting such an enquiry" (St. Patrick, March 17th).

From a patriotic point of view it might be urged that, although innumerable books and pamphlets have been written on our subject, not one too many has seen the light, inasmuch as each of them has served in a greater or lesser degree to keep the memory of our great Apostle ever fresh in our minds.

We are deeply indebted to the Rev. Professor Leilleux, who is at present engaged in writing a "History of the Diocese of Boulogne-sur-Mer," and to the Abbe Massot, chaplain to the Little Sisters of the Poor in that town, for having clearly proved to us that ancient Bononia was called "Bonauen," and Caligula's tower—Turris Ordinis—was called "Nemtor" by the Gaulish Celts. These discoveries go far to show that the Apostle of Ireland was a native of ancient Bononia, now called Boulogne-sur-Mer.

Colgan, who published his "Trias Thaumaturga" in 1647, assures us in his fifth Appendix, chapter i., that there was an old tradition in Armorica that St. Patrick was a native of that province; and the same author adds that several Irish writers adhered to that opinion. This book, therefore, does not seek to formulate a new theory; its only object is to gather together many of the records which tend to prove that St. Patrick was born in Armorican Britain.

Our most grateful thanks are also due to the Very Rev. Canon Gildea, D.D., M.R., who has kindly read through this book for the "Nil obstat"; and to the courteous Curator of the Library and Museum at Boulogne for permitting us to make a sketch of Caligula's famous tower and lighthouse, which was called Turris Ordinis or Turris Ardens by the Romans, and Nemtor or Nemthur by the Armorican Britons.

WILLIAM CANON FLEMING.

ST. MARY'S, MOORFIELDS,
LONDON, E.C.

ST. MARY'S, MOORFIELDS,
LONDON, E.C.

# CONTENTS

# ST. PATRICK'S PARENTAGE.

ABOUT the middle of the fourth century a noble decurion named Calphurnius espoused Conchessa, the niece of St. Martin of Tours. Heaven blessed their union with several children, the youngest of whom was a boy, who received at his baptism the name of Succath, which in the Gaelic tongue signifies "valiant."

Jocelin is responsible for the statement that the parents of the future Apostle of Ireland took, by mutual consent, the vow of celibacy after St. Patrick's birth, and that Calphurnius, like St. Gregory of Nyssa, St. Hilary, and St. Germanus, who were all married men, "closed his days in the priesthood" (chap, ii., p. 2). "There were thousands of priests and Bishops," as Dr. Dollinger observes, "who had sons before their ordination" ("History of the Church," vol. ii., p. 23, note).

There are others, however, like Father Bullen Morris, who are of opinion that St. Patrick's declaration in the "Confession" that his father was "a deacon" is a mistake on the part of the copyist for "decurion," and, as a proof of this contention, they point to the words made use of by the Saint in his Epistle to Coroticus, which is admittedly genuine: "I am of noble blood, for my father was a decurion. I have bartered my nobility—for which I feel neither shame nor sorrow—for the sake of others." It is difficult to reconcile this statement with the assurance given in the "Confession" that his father was a humble deacon. "It is inconceivable," as Father Bullen Morris argues, "that the Saint, sprung from a noble family, should base his claim to nobility on the fact that his father, Calphurnius, was a deacon. On the other hand, the theory that Calphurnius was a Roman officer fits in with both statements of the Saint" ("St. Patrick, Apostle of Ireland," p. 285, Appendix).

The same author gives another reason for calling in question this part of the text of the "Confession" in the "Book of Armagh." A scribe made an addition to the genealogy of St. Patrick as recorded in the Book, writing on the margin "Son of Odisseus"; and these words are actually introduced into the text by Dr. Whitley Stokes, in his edition of the "Confession," without either note or comment. It is easy to imagine, therefore, that ancient Celtic writers, with their passion for genealogies, should tamper with the ancestors of St. Patrick. Nicholson, a distinguished Irish scholar, was, of opinion that the addition "a deacon" was mere guesswork on the part of the copyist, and wrote "incertus liber hic"—"the book is here unreliable" ("St. Patrick, Apostle of Ireland," Appendix, pp. 286—288).

Moreover, if the word "a deacon" in the "Book of Armagh" is the true reading, it must surely be a matter for surprise that St. Patrick, who sternly enforced the law of celibacy in Ireland as part of the discipline of the Catholic Church, should describe himself as the son of a deacon without either comment or explanation, and more especially when we remember that the Council of Elvira, A.D. 305, and the Council of Aries, A.D. 314, had enforced the laws of celibacy—"The severe discipline of the Councils of Elvira and Aries," writes Alzog, "obtained the force of law and became general throughout the Western Church" ("Universal Church History," vol. i., chap, iv., pp. 280, 281). The practice of clerical celibacy, therefore, existed in the Western Church probably before Calphurnius was born, and certainly before he was old enough to get married.

Calphurnius was admittedly a decurion, or Roman officer. Now Pope Innocent I., in his Letter to Exuperius, Bishop of Toulouse, in the year 405, in answer to a number of questions submitted to him by the Bishop, stated that there was an impediment to the ordination of men who had served in the army on account of the loose morality prevalent in the camp. As the Pope was simply laying down the rules of discipline already existing in the Church, Calphurnius, being a Roman officer, could not have been ordained without the removal of the impediment. All this tends at least to prove that we should read "decurion" for "deacon" in the "Confession."

According to the "Book of Sligo," St. Patrick was born on Wednesday (373), baptized on Wednesday, and died on Wednesday, March 17th, A.D. 493.

# THE DIFFERENT BIRTHPLACES ASSIGNED TO ST. PATRICK

BARONIUS and Matthew of Westminster declare that St. Patrick was born in Ireland, but scarcely any writer of the present day ventures to express that view. O'Sullivan, Keating, Lanigan, and many French writers contend that he was a native of Armoric Gaul, or Britain in France. Welshmen are strongly of opinion that Ross Vale, Pembrokeshire, was the honoured place; whilst Canon Sylvester Malone attributed the glory to Burrium, Monmouthshire, a town situated, as Camden narrates, near the spot where the River Brydhin empties itself into the Usk. The Scholiast, Colgan, and Archbishop Healy seem to have no doubt as to the Saint's birth at Dumbarton. Ware believes that a town that once stood almost under the shadow of the crag possessed a stronger claim; Usher and the Aberdeen Breviary are equally positive that Kilpatrick was the town. Cardinal Moran, on the other hand, has convinced himself that St. Patrick first saw the light of day at a place that once stood near the present town of Hamilton, just where the river Avon discharges itself into the Clyde. Some English writers have strongly advocated the claims of a Roman town named Bannaventa that once stood near the present site of Davantry, Northamptonshire. Professor Bury, in his "Life of St. Patrick," had the doubtful honour of inventing a new birthplace for the Saint; he tells us that St. Patrick was born at a Bannaventa, "which was probably situated in the regions of the Lower Severn."

## ST. PATRICK WAS NOT BORN IN WALES.

The belief that St. Patrick was born in Ross Vale, Pembrokeshire, is founded principally on the supposed acceptance of that view by Camden, and on an old tradition to the effect that St. Patrick, having completed his missionary labours in Ireland, founded a monastery at Menevia and died there.

As the authority of the learned Camden carries with it great weight, it will here be not out of place to quote his own declaration, which is as follows: "Beyond Ross Vale is a spacious promontory called by Ptolemy Octopitarum, by the Britons Pebidiog and Kantev-Dewi, and by the English St. David's land. . . . It was the retiring place and nursery of several Saints, for Calphurnius, a British priest—*as some have written, I know not hew truly*—begot there St. Patrick, the Apostle of Ireland" ("Britannia," vol. ii., p. 32). The same author, in another place, gives expression to his own views on the subject, to which, indeed, he does not seem to have devoted very serious study. "St. Patrick," he writes, "was a Briton born in Clydesdale, and related to St. Martin, Bishop of Tours, and he was a disciple of St. Germanus"

("Britannia," vol. ii., p. 326).

The Ross Vale theory has, in truth, as little in its favour as the old, but groundless, tradition that St. Patrick founded a monastery and ended his days at Menevia. This is plainly contradicted by the Saint's assertion that after he had landed as a missionary in Ireland he never once left, and ended his days in the land of his adoption. "Though I could have wished to leave them" (the Irish), writes the Saint in his "Confession," "and had been desirous of going to Britain, as if to my own country and parents, and not that alone, but even to Gaul to visit my brethren, and see the face of the Lord's Saints. But I am bound in the spirit, and He who witnesseth all will account me guilty if I do it, and I fear to lose the labour which I have begun; and not I, but the Lord Christ, who commanded me to come and remain with them for the rest of my life, if the Lord prolongs it, and keeps me from all sin before Him." This statement, which was made by St. Patrick just before his death, when he wrote the "Confession," could never have been volunteered if he had once left the country where the Lord had commanded him to remain for the rest of his life.

## THE SCOTCH THEORIES ON THIS SUBJECT.

The Scholiast and Colgan, who identify the Crag of Dumbarton with the Nemthur of the Saint's nativity, are faced by the unanswerable difficulty that though Nemthur may be the name of a tower, or may be the name of the district in which the tower stood, it cannot be the name of a town. The Saint in his "Confession" states that his father hailed from the suburban district of a town called Bonaven Tabernise, where he possessed a country seat, from which he (the Saint) was carried off into captivity. Bonaven, therefore, is rightly regarded as St. Patrick's native town. St. Fiacc simply states that St. Patrick was born at Nemthur, but he does not assart that Nemthur was a town, otherwise he would be at variance with his Patron, who plainly gives us to understand that he was born at Bonaven Tabernise, The only way of reconciling this apparent conflict of evidence is to assume that St. Fiacc is giving the name either of the tower or the district in which St. Patrick was born, while the Saint is giving the name of the town of which he was a native, but not the name of the district which was honoured by his birth.

Dr. Lanigan, however, objects "that no sensible writer, wishing to inform his readers where the Saint was born, would say that he came into the world in a tower" ("Eccl. Hist.," vol. i., p. 101).

Nemthur may indeed be a corruption of Neustria, as Dr. Lanigan suggests; but it must not be forgotten that districts not unfrequently derive their names from famous monuments that either stand or have stood in their midst. We have an illustration of this in the very locality where many believe that St. Patrick was born. The high level on the north-eastern cliff's of Boulogne is called even at the present time "Tour d'Ordre," deriving its name from Caligula's tower, which the Romans called Turris Ordinis, and the Gaulish Celts called Nemtor, which once stood on the lofty plateau, but is no longer in existence.

Ware's theory, in his own words, is this: "I must dissent from the Scholiast that Nemthur and Alcuid were the same place; though it must be granted that they stood near each other, as appears from a passage of Jocelin: 'there was a promontory hanging over the town of Empthor, a certain fortification, the ruins of which are yet visible,' and a little later: 'this celebrated place, seated in the valley of the Clyde, is, in the language of the country, called "Dunbreaton," that is, the Fort of the Britons'" (Ware, vol. i., p. 6).

Relying also on Jocelin's statement that Tabernise signified a "Field of Tents"—"Tabernaculorum Campus"—and on his unwarranted assertion that the habitation of Calphurnius was "not far from the Irish Sea," Usher pointed out Kilpatrick, a town situated between Dumbarton and the city of Glasgow, as St. Patrick's native town.

Jocelin's "Life of St. Patrick," as Canon O'Hanlon has said, is "incomparably the worst" of the Latin lives of the Saint, and yet it is on this untrustworthy foundation, and on the contradictions of the Scholiast, that Usher and Ware rest their respective theories. Usher discovered a Roman camp at Kilpatrick, and found that the town was "not far from the Irish Sea," and it is upon this weak hypothesis that the Kilpatrick theory rests.

The Aberdeen Breviary coincides with Usher, and the lesson referring to St. Patrick is as follows: "St. Patrick, the Apostle of Ireland, was born of Calphurnius, a man of illustrious Celtic descent, and of Conchessa, a native of Gaul and a sister of St. Martin, Bishop of Tours. He was conceived with many miraculous signs at Dumbarton Castle, but was born and reared at Kilpatrick in Scotland, near the Castle."

But if the Aberdeen Breviary asserts that St. Patrick was born at Kilpatrick, the Continental Breviaries, as Colgan freely admits, are equally positive that he was a native of Armoric Gaul.

Cardinal Moran, in an article contributed to the *Dublin Review* in the spring of 1880, insisted rightly that the solution of the difficulty is to be found in the word Bonaven. Bon, or Ban, he tells us, is a Celtic word which signifies the mouth of a river, and Avon is the river itself. From this, he argues that the Saint was born at a town which once stood on the present site of Hamilton, which is situated at the mouth of the Avon, just where that river discharges itself into the Clyde. The same argument would apply with equal force to a town situated at the mouth of the River Aven on the French coast, which flows into the harbour of Concarneu in Brittany.

Anyone who accepts the authority of Probus, who asserts that Bonaven Tabernise "was not far from the Western sea," or of the Scholiast, who is the author of the Dumbarton theory, will see a grave objection to accepting the Cardinal's solution of the problem: Hamilton is about fifty miles distant from Dumbarton, and far away from the Atlantic Ocean.

None of the authors mentioned make any attempt to reconcile the two contradictory statements of the Scholiast: (1) that St. Patrick was born at Dumbarton, and (2) that he was captured in Armorica. They have failed to notice that, if the Saint was captured in Armorica, he could not have been born at Dumbarton, because he assures us in his "Confession" that he was captured at his father's home. Even according to the admissions of the Scholiast, therefore, Bonaven Tabernise, St. Patrick's home, was situated in Armorica. Usher, Ware, and Cardinal Moran, while contending that the Apostle of Ireland was born in North Britain, refuse to accept the Scholiast's statement that he was a native of Dumbarton.

## ST. PATRICK WAS NOT BORN IN GREAT BRITAIN.

Ignoring altogether both the Scotch and Welsh theories as to the birthplace of St. Patrick, Professor Bury, in his Life of the Saint, holds that Ireland's Apostle was born in a village named Bannaventa; not, however, Bannaventa now known as Daventry in Northamptonshire, seeing that that town would be too far "from the Western sea," but another Bannaventa somewhere on the sea coast, and "perhaps in the region of the Severn" (chap, ii., p. 17, and Appendix, 323).

The whole of Professor Bury's new theory rests on a very faint similarity between Bonaven or Bannaven—the name which the Saint gives to the town of his birth—and Bannaventa; and on an entirely gratuitous assumption that there must have been a town named Bannaventa "in the regions of the lower Severn."

Professor Bury is recognised as a very able historian by the literary world; his Appendix alone to the "Life of St. Patrick" affords ample proof of his learning and genius. Nevertheless, he occasionally indulges in some obiter dicta without historical proof, and at times lays himself open to the charge of want of historical accuracy. For instance, he ascribes the origin of the Papal power to a decree of the Emperor Valintinian III., issued in A.D. 445 at the instance of Pope Leo, which is supposed to have conferred "on the Bishop of Rome sovran authority in the Western provinces which were under the imperial sway." Before that period, he tells us, "the Roman See was recognised by imperial decrees of Valintinian I. and Gratian as a Court to which the clergy might appeal from the decisions of Provincial Councils in any part of the Western portion of the Empire"; that "the answers to such were called Decretals"; that there were no Decretals before those of Damasus (366, 384); "that those who consulted the Roman Pontiff were not bound in any way to accept his ruling"; and that when Pope Zosimus endeavoured to enforce his Decretals "he was smitten on one cheek by the Synods of Africa; he was smitten on the other by the Gallic Bishops at the Council of Turin." "By tact and adroitness," Pope Leo induced the Emperor Valintinian III. to issue an edict which established the Papal power over the Western provinces of the Roman Empire. The Professor explains how Ireland, on account of its geographical position, was drawn into the Roman Confederation; and it is on that account that he admits the genuineness of the decree of a Synod held by St. Patrick, to the effect that in cases of ecclesiastical difficulties, which the Irish Bishops could not solve themselves, the Sovereign Pontiff should be asked to give a decision ("Life of St. Patrick," pp. 59—66).

The Professor's perversion of ecclesiastical history is a blot on his otherwise excellent "Life of St. Patrick." How can he reconcile these statements with St. Clement's Epistle to the Corinthians, which Eusebius admits to be genuine, or with Pope Stephen's exercise of pontifical authority in the case of St. Cyprian and the question of validity of baptism conferred by heretics; or with the celebrated declaration of St. Irenaeus on the authority of the Church of Rome, which is as follows: "It is a matter of necessity that every Church should agree with this Church on account of its pre-eminent authority, that is, the faithful of all nations"? ("Irenseus contra Hereses," vol. L, lib. iii., cap. iii., sect. 2, translated by Rev. A. Roberts, Edinburgh, 1868). Now St. Clement lived in Apostolic times, St. Cyprian from 200 to 258, and St. Irenaeus flourished between A.D. 150 to 202, while the Roman Emperors were persecuting the Church. Leaving the well-defined path of history, the Professor indulges in speculations which will seem to most people to be without warrant.

St. Patrick's home, he tells us, was in "a village named Bannaventa, but we cannot with any certainty identify its locality. The only Bannaventa that we know lays near Daventry; but this position does not agree with an ancient indication that the village of Calphurnius was close to the Western sea. As the two elements of the name Bannaventa were probably not uncommon in British geographical nomenclature, it is not rash to suppose that there were other small places so called besides the only Bannaventa that happens to appear in Roman geographical sources, and we may be inclined to look for the Bannaventa of Calphurnius in South-Western Britain, perhaps in the regions of the lower Severn. The village must have been in the neighbourhood of a town in possession of a municipal council of decurions" (chap, ii., pp. 16, 17).

The Professor quietly assumes without proof that Bonaven and Bannaventa are one and the same; that "vicus" is used in its secondary meaning of "a village," and not in its primary signification, "a district or quarter of a town," in the "Confession"; and while admitting that there was no other town in Britain named Bannaventa except Bannaventa in Northampton, as far as can be gathered from "Roman sources of information," and passing over the fact that Camden's "Britannia," which gives the history of every old town in the kingdom, and Horsley's "Britannia Romana," which performs the same task, make no mention of any other Bannaventa, whilst old maps and itineraries are equally silent, the Professor seemingly rests satisfied with his own mere conjecture, that there may have been another Bannaventa, which was probably situated in the regions of the lower Severn. Surely a speculation of this kind may well be called unwarranted.

## ST. PATRICK WAS A NATIVE OF ARMORIC GAUL.

Colgan, when he published his "Trias Thaumaturga" in 1647, admitted that there was "A constant tradition amongst the inhabitants of that country that St. Patrick was a native of Armorican Britain, which tradition several Irishmen endorse," (In Britannia Armorica regione Gallise natum esse vetus est traditio incolarum istius terrae cui nonulli suffragantur Hiberni.) (Appendix 5, p. 2.)

Don Philip O'Sullivan, who published "Patriciana Decas" in 1621, strongly upheld this view. Attempts, however, have more recently been made to prove that St. Patrick was a native of Scotland, but there undoubtedly existed a tradition in favour of the belief that St. Patrick came from Gaul to Ireland, and this view is firmly held by Keating and Lanigan, two of our ablest Irish historians.

St. Patrick narrates in his "Confession" that he was born in the suburbs of a town called Bonaven, where there was a Roman encampment, and that, when a youth in his fifteenth year, he was taken prisoner by the Irish Scots, "the nation to whom he showed tender forgiveness." The very year of his capture corresponds with the raid of Niall of the Nine Hostages into Armorica. As the Irish Scots invaded that country just when St. Patrick had attained his fifteenth year, and as the Saint declared that he had been taken prisoner by men of the nation which he had converted, it is more than probable that he was taken prisoner during that raid.

As Bononia, or Boulogne-sur-Mer, was called Bonauen by the Gaulish Celts, and as the "v" and "u" are convertible in Gaelic, the Bonauen of the Gaulish Celts and the Bonaven of St. Patrick's "Confession" may well be one and the same place. Indeed, there are arguments which seem to place their identity beyond reasonable doubt.

St. Fiacc declares that the Apostle of Ireland was born at Nemthur. Now, Nemtor was the name given by the Gaulish Celts to Caligula's tower in the suburbs, and close to the City of Bononia, or Boulogne. St. Fiacc, therefore, gives the name of the district—for the district about Nemthur was named after the prominent landmark in its midst, and St. Patrick the name of the town in the suburbs of which he was born.

According to the Celtic legend, Calphurnius was a Roman officer in charge of the tower, and was slain on the occasion when his son Patrick was made prisoner by the Irish Scots.

A close examination, however, of the "Confession" and of the old Latin lives of the Saint, will, it seems to us, securely determine which of the four theories—the Scotch, the Welsh, the English, or the French—concerning St. Patrick's native country, carried with it the greatest amount of probability.

# BONAVEN TABERNIAE WAS WELL KNOWN TO THE IRISH SCOTS

THIS will appear evident from a close study of the "Confession": "Ego Patritius, peccator, rustissimus et minimus omnium fidelium, et contemptabilissimus apud plurimos, patrem habui Calphurnium diaconum, filium quondam Potiti, presbyteri, qui fuit vico Bonaven Taberniae, villulam enim prope habuit ubi ego in capturam dedi. Annorum tune eram fere XVI."

"I, Patrick, a sinner, the most uncultured and humblest of all the Faithful, and, in the eyes of many, the most contemptible, had for father Calphurnius, a deacon, and the son of Potitus, a priest, who hailed from the suburbs of Bonaven, where the encampment stood, for he possessed a little country seat close by, from whence I was taken captive when I had almost attained my sixteenth year."

The primary meaning of "vicus" is a district, or a quarter of a city, and "villula" signifies "a little country seat" (Smith's "Latin and English Dictionary"). The district of the city of Bonaven alluded to was evidently suburban, because the house in which Calphurnius and his family dwelt was a "little country seat," which was, nevertheless, close to ("prope") the town.

The Saint must have had some special reason for writing the name of his native town in Gaelic, while the rest of the "Confession" is written in Latin. There was a very important town in Armorican Britain at the time, which was called Bononia by the Romans, and Bonauen by the Gaulish Celts (Hersart de la Villemarque Celtic Legend, pp. 3, 4). In the days of Julius Caesar its harbour was called Portus Ictius ("Dictionnaire Archeologique et Historique du Pas de Calais").

O'Donovan, who translated the "Annals of the Kingdom of Ireland by the Four Masters," assures us in a note, under the year 405, that Niall of the Nine Hostages was assassinated by the banished Prince Eochaidh at Muir N'Icht, which the translator identifies as Bononia, or Boulogne-sur-Mer. Keating, on the other hand, narrates that King Niall received his mortal wound on the banks of the Loire. It is easy to reconcile the apparent difference between the two accounts, if we assume that the wounded Monarch was carried in a dying state to join the fleet which lay at anchor in the fine bay which then formed the outer harbour of Boulogne, and that he had at least the consolation of dying on board his own ship.

Muir N'Icht, or Portus Ictius, then possessed the finest harbour in northern Gaul. From the days of Julius Caesar, Portus Ictius, or the harbour of Boulogne, was the port from which the Roman troops sailed to Britain, and the harbour to which they steered on their return. On top of Caligula's tower there was a lighthouse for the guidance of vessels at sea. The very fact that King Niall made use of this harbour when he raided Armorica in the twenty-seventh year of his reign, makes it likely that he sailed into the same harbour when first invading that country in the ninth year of his reign. The sons of the soldiers who took part in the second raid were still alive; and the memories of both expeditions were still fresh in the minds of the brave Irish Scots when St. Patrick wrote his "Confession."

The records of both expeditions were undoubtedly read at the annual Feast of Tara, when the Kings, nobles and learned were accustomed to meet annually and examine the National records (Keating, pp. 337—388).

The triumphant march of devastation made by the Irish Monarch in the ninth year of his reign, when he led his troops "from the walls of Antoninus to the shores of Kent"; the successful raid into Armorica which commenced with the capture of the Roman encampment at Haute Ville, Boulogne, and ended in the plundering of the surrounding country, must have been the burden of many a warlike song whenever the Irish minstrels chanted the glorious triumphs of King Niall's invincible troops. It is, therefore, but natural to suppose every man, woman, and child in Ireland had often heard the name of Bonaven, where the soldiers of King Niall stormed the encampment, and where the ever-conquering Monarch expired.

St. Patrick, who, according to the "Scholiast," the Fifth and Tripartite Lives, and Heating's "History" (p. 312), was captured in Armorica, and who, according to Hersart de la Villemarque and Dr. Lanigan, was taken captive at Boulogne, was well aware that every Irishman would know the town to which he was referring when he declared in his "Confession" that his father, Calphurnius, and consequently he himself, hailed from the suburban district of Bonaven Taberniae, or Bononia, where the Roman encampment stood.

# HISTORY OF THE TOWN BONAVEN, OR BONONIA

THE ancient records of Bononia, or Boulogne-sur-Mer, date back to about half a century before Christ—to the time when Julius Caesar, anticipating Napoleon the Great, stood on the north-eastern cliffs of that town gazing through the Channel mist on the dim outline of that Britain which he had resolved to subjugate.

At that period two headlands stretched out into the sea for a distance of three miles—one on the northeastern side of the town, near to what is now known as Fort la Cresche; and the other from Cape Alpreck, about three miles lower down on the south-western coast. These headlands, stretching out into the sea, so encircled a bay as to form it into an outward haven.

The inner harbour of Boulogne was approached by a narrow channel dividing the north-eastern from the south-western cliffs; and the waters of the bay, flowing through it and uniting with the River Liane in covering the present site of the lower town, rushed onwards as far as the valley of Tintelleries and the vale of St. Martin.

Facing the site of the present town there was an island called Elna, and on it was built the ancient town of Gessoriac, which was connected with the mainland by a bridge. Realising the future importance of the place both for naval and military purposes, Caesar commissioned Pedius, a native of Bononia, in Italy, to lay out a town on the declivity of the Grande Rue, leading to Haute Ville, as the upper town and the hill leading to it are called at the present day. (Bertrand's "History of Boulogne-sur-Mer," pp. 17, 18. "Walkernaer's Geography," vol. i., p. 454).

The walls of the present fortifications of Haute Ville, built in the thirteenth century, rest on the ancient foundations of the old Roman encampment. This fact was proved at the time when a tunnelling was made for the railway from Boulogne to Calais under Haute Ville ("Dictionnaire Historique et Archeologique du Pas de Calais," vol. i, p. 22). The circuit of the present fortifications, about 700 yards square, present to-day the appearance pf the old Roman encampment. "The camp of a Roman legion," writes Gibbon, "presented all the appearance of a fortified city. As soon as the place was marked out, the pioneers carefully levelled the ground and removed every impediment that might interrupt its perfect regularity. It forms an exact quadrangle, and we might calculate that a square of 700 yards was sufficient for the encampment of 20,000 Romans, though a similar number of our troops would expose to an enemy a front of more than treble its extent. In the midst of the camp the pretorium, or general's quarters, rose above the others;

the cavalry, the infantry, and the auxiliaries occupied their respective stations; the streets were broad and straight, and a vacant of 200 feet was left on all sides between the tents and the ramparts. The rampart itself was usually twelve feet high, and defended by a ditch twelve feet in depth, as well as in breadth. This important labour was performed by the legionaries themselves, to whom the use of the spade and the pick-axe was no less familiar than the sword and the pilum" ("Decline and Fall of the Roman Empire," vol. i., p. 27.) This gives a faithful description of the Roman encampment (Castra Stativa) at Boulogne, which is described by St. Patrick as Bonaven Tabernise, or Bononia, where the Roman encampment was pitched. Bononia, according to Bertrand's "History of Boulogne," was regarded by the Romans as their "principal dockyard" in Northern Gaul; and Suetonius, in his "Lives of the Twelve Caesars," describes it "as the port from which the Roman legions successively departed for Britain" (p. 283, note).

Many err in supposing that Gessoriac and Bononia were one and the same town, originally called Gessoriac, and later, that is to say during the reign of Constantine the Great, known as Bononia. It is true, however, that during that Emperor's reign Gessoriac also came to be called Bononia.

It is well to observe that the Morini, or inhabitants of the coast in the neighbourhood of Boulogne, were converted to Christianity by St. Firmin about the close of the second century; and that St. Fusian built a chapel on the banks of the River Liane, which flows through Boulogne, in the year 275.

St. Patrick, in his "Confession," represents himself and the fellow-citizens of his youth as Christians who had not observed the Commandments of God, and who had not been obedient to their priests. At that time the Northern Britons were pagans; St. Ninian, who flourished about the year 400, was the first missioner who preached the Gospel to the Dalraida and Southern Picts. They could not, therefore, have been described in the year 388, when St. Patrick was made captive, as Christians who had ceased to practise their religion. "I knew not the real God," writes St. Patrick, "and I was brought captive to Ireland with many thousand men, as we deserved, for we had forgotten God and had not kept His Commandments, and were disobedient to our priests, who admonished us for our salvation. And the Lord brought down upon us the anger of His Spirit, and scattered us amongst many nations, even to the ends of the earth, where now my humble self may be witnessed among strangers" ("Confession").

# ST. PATRICK MADE CAPTIVE BY NIALL
## OF THE NINE HOSTAGES

GIBBON narrates that about the middle of the fourth century the "sea coast of Gaul and Britain were exposed to the depredations of the Saxons" (vol. i., P- 739); and Bertrand, in his "History of Boulogne," admits that the city was plundered by the Saxons in the year 371, but that the invaders spared Caligula's tower and lighthouse on account of its usefulness for their safe navigation. The silence of local history concerning two raids made by the Irish Scots into Armorica in the years 388 and 402 is not surprising, seeing that French writers admit that there is practically no history of Armorica or more than a century after the Saxon raid in the year 371. Gibbon, however, in his history of the "Decline and Fall of the Roman Empire," narrates that "the hostile tribes of the North, who detested the pride and power of the King of the World, suspended their domestic feuds, and the barbarians of the land and sea, the Picts, the Scots, and the Saxons, spread themselves with rapid and irresistible fury from the walls of Antoninus to the shores of Kent" (vol. i., p. 744). Keating supplements this information by describing the two raids made by the Irish Scots into Armorica; the first of which took place in the year 388, and the second in 402, or about that time. This Irish historian is considered by Professor Stokes to be a most trustworthy authority. "Keating," writes the Professor, "had access to the Munster Documents, which are now lost. He gives a long account of the Irish invasions of England and France exactly corresponding to the statements of the Roman historian, Amianus Marcellinus, and to the 'Annals of the Four Masters'" ("Ireland and the Celtic Church," p. 38, note).

Of the raids of King Niall into Armorica the first is the more interesting, for it proves, first, that St. Patrick was born in the year 373, and, next, that he was captured neither in North Britain, nor Wales, but in Armorican Britain.

To escape from these conclusions, Doctor Lanigan, who held that St. Patrick was born in the year 387, writes as follows: "I find in Keating but one expedition of Niall to the coast of Gaul, during which he says, in another place, that St. Patrick with two hundred of the noblest youth were brought away. . . . This event occurred in the latter end of Niall Naoigiallach's reign, and not as early as the ninth year of it. . . . We have no authority," continues Lanigan, "for his having visited Gaul at any time until the period already given, and which is clearly marked in Irish history. Our Saint's captivity may be assigned to 403, and to a time not long prior to King Niall's death. Thus the date of his birth and captivity, considering the circumstances now mentioned, help to confirm each other, and, combined with his age at consecration, authorizes his birth in 387" ("Eccl. Hist, of Ireland," vol. i., pp.

137, 138).

Contrary to what Dr. Lanigan has just stated, a close study of Keating's "History" will prove that King Niall made two raids into Armorica, the first in the ninth and the second in the twenty-seventh year of his reign, and the account of the two expeditions is clear and unmistakable. "There is an old manuscript in vellum, exceedingly curious, entitled 'The Life of St. Patrick,' which treats likewise of the lives of Muchuda Albain and other Saints, from which I," writes Keating, "shall transcribe a citation that relates to St. Patrick.

"Patrick was a Briton born and descended from religious parents," and in the same place is the following remark: "The Irish Scots, under Niall the King, wasted and destroyed many provinces in Britain in opposition to the power of the Romans. They attempted to possess themselves of the northern part of Britain, and, at length, having driven out the old inhabitants, these Irish seized upon the country and settled in it." The same author (of the manuscript) upon this occasion remarks that from henceforth Great Britain was divided into three kingdoms, that were distinguished by the names of Scotia, Anglia, and Britia.

This ancient writer likewise asserts that when Niall, the hero of the Nine Hostages, undertook the expedition for settling the tribe of the Dailraida in Scotland, the Irish fleet sailed to the place where St. Patrick resided; "At this time the fleet out of Ireland plundered the country in which St. Patrick then lived, and, according to the custom of the Irish, many captives were carried away from thence, among whom was St. Patrick, in the sixteenth year of his age, and his two sisters, Lupida and Darerca; and St. Patrick was led captive into Ireland in the *ninth* year of the reign of Niall, King of Ireland, who was the mighty monarch of the kingdom for seven-and-twenty years, and brought away spoils out of England, Britain, and France."

"By this expression it is supposed," continues Keating, "that Niall of the Nine Hostages waged war against Britain or Wales, and perhaps made a conquest of the country; *and it is more than probable* that, when the Irish Prince had finished his design upon the kingdom of Wales, he carried his arms in a fleet to France and invaded the country at the time called Armorica, but now Little Brittany, and from thence he led St. Patrick and his two sisters into captivity.

"And this I am rather induced to believe, because the mother of St. Patrick was sister of St. Martin, the Bishop of Tours in France; and *I have read in an ancient Irish manuscript, whose authority I cannot dispute, that St. Patrick and his two sisters were brought captive into Ireland from Armorica, or Brittany,* in the kingdom of France. It is evident likewise that when Niall, the King of Ireland, had succeeded with the Britons, he despatched a formidable fleet to plunder the coast of France, and succeeded; and that he carried away numbers of captives with him into captivity, one of which, it is reasonable to suppose, was the young Patrick, who was afterwards distinguished by the name of the Irish Saint.

"Niall, encouraged by the number of his captives and the success of his arms in France, *resolved upon another expedition,* and accordingly raised a grand army of his Irish subjects for that purpose, and sent a commission to the General of the

Dalraida in Scotland to follow him with his choicest troops and assist him in the invasion. Niall having prepared a sufficient number of transports and a full supply of provisions, weighed anchor with his victorious Irish, and *steering his course directly to France*, had the advantage of a prosperous wind, and in a few days landed upon the coast. He immediately set himself to spoil and ravage the country near the river Loire. Here it was that the General of the Dalraida found him, and both armies being joined, they committed dreadful hostilities, which obliged the inhabitants to fly and leave the country to the mercy of the invaders.

"The commanding officer of the Dalraida in this expedition was Gabhran, the son of Dombanguirt, who brought over with him Eochaidh, the son of Ena Cinsalach, King of Leinster. This young Prince had been formerly banished into Scotland by Niall, but resolving to be revenged when opportunity offered, he desired to be admitted as a volunteer in the service, and was by that means transported into France. The King of Ireland being informed of his arrival, would on no account permit him to visit him, nor suffer him in his presence. But Eochaidh soon found an opportunity to execute his design; for one day, perceiving the King sitting on the banks of the Loire, he hid himself secretly in an opposite grove on the other side, and shot Niall through the body with an arrow; the wound was mortal, and he died instantly" ("General History of Ireland," pp. 311—313). According to O'Donovan's translation of "Muir N'Icht," Niall lived long enough to reach his fleet at Boulogne, where he expired.

Notwithstanding, then, Lanigan's positive assertion, it is quite evident from Keating's history that King Niall twice invaded Armorica; first, after he had devastated the Island of Britain in the ninth year of his reign, when St. Patrick was captured, and again in the twenty-seventh year of his reign, when he sailed directly from Ireland to Gaul and expired at Boulogne.

The events may be briefly stated as follows: Niall succeeded Criomthan in the year 376. In the ninth year of his reign, or A.D. 385, he prepared an expedition against the Picts, who were harassing the Scots settlers in North Britain. Having completed his task, he overran England, and finished his raid by crossing over to Armorica, before returning triumphant to Ireland with St. Patrick amongst his captives.

Now St. Patrick, who was born in the year 373, passed his thirteenth and fourteenth years while King Niall was chastising the Picts in Scotland and ravaging Britain; but he had reached his fifteenth year in the year 388, when the Irish fleet sailed from Armorica to Ireland. The words of the Saint in his Epistle to Coroticus: "Have I not tender mercy towards the nation which formerly took me captive," place the Saint's capture by the Irish Scots beyond doubt, whilst they confirm Keating's declaration that King Niall captured St. Patrick in his first raid to Armorica.

The capture of the Saint in Armorica is confirmed by the Scholiast, by the Tripartite Life, and by Probus. St. Patrick, as we have already seen, was captured while residing at his father's "villula" in the suburban district of Bonaven Tabernise, or Bononia, where the Roman encampment stood. This account harmonises with the "Celtic Legend," which narrates that at that period, "when Bononia was invaded by the Irish pirates, a mutiny broke out among the soldiers in the encampment, which rendered the city an easy prey to the invaders. Calphurnius, the Roman officer defending Caligula's tower, was slain, and his son Patrick was carried into captivity" ("La Legende Celtique per le Vicomte Hersart de la Villemarque," p. 8).

According to the "Book of Sligo," as has been seen already, the Apostle of Ireland first saw the light of day on Wednesday, April 5th; not on Wednesday, April 5th, 372, as Usher imagined, for, as Ware points out, April 5th did not fall on Wednesday, 372, but on Wednesday, 373. There is overwhelming evidence to prove that St. Patrick died in the year 493, having attained the 120th year of his age. Usher, Ware, the Tripartite Life, the "Vita Secunda," the "Vita Quarta," the "Leabhar Braec," the "Annals of the Four Masters," the "Annals of Innisfail," the "Book of Howth," the "Annals of Tigernasch," the "Chronicon Scotorum," the "Annals of Boyle," Marianus Scotus, Nennius, Geraldus Cambrensis, Florence of Worcester, and Roger of Wendover all maintain this. The year of the Saint's birth may, therefore, be accurately obtained by subtracting 120 from 493, the date of his death. This process will show that St. Patrick was born in 373, and captured in the very year of King Niall's raid into Armorica, 388, when the Saint had attained his fifteenth year.

The great age of the Saint at the time of his death, although marvellous, is not incredible. In Chambers' "Book of Days," quoted by. Father Bullen Morris, instances are given of 2,003 centenarians, 17 of whom lived 150 years. Father Montalto, a Jesuit, who was born in 1689, was present at the Church of the Gensu at Rome in the 125th year of his age, when Pius VII. re-established the Society of Jesus. In 1881 the photograph of Gabriel Salivar was sent to the Vatican as the oldest inhabitant of the world. It was proved on convincing evidence that he had reached 150 years. Thomas Parr, as is well known, attained the age of 152 years and nine months before he bade adieu to the world.

# ST. PATRICK AFTER HIS CAPTIVITY
# RETURNS TO (GAUL)
# HIS NATIVE COUNTRY

"AND on a certain night I heard in sleep a voice saying to me: 'Thou fasteth well; fasting thou shalt return to thy own native country'" (patria). "And again, after a little, I heard a response, saying to me: 'Behold thy ship is ready'" (St. Patrick's "Confession").

St. Fiacc suggests, Probus asserts, and Professor Bury admits that St. Patrick, after his captivity, fled to Gaul, and not to Great Britain. Gaul, therefore, and not the Island of Britain, was St. Patrick's native land.

If either Northern or Southern Britain were St. Patrick's native country, it seems incredible that the-Saint should be required to travel a distance of 200 Roman miles, from the North-East to the West of Ireland, in order to embark for Britain, when Lough Larne is but 30 nautical miles from Scotland,, and not more than 15 miles from Mount Slemish, and while Belfast and Strangford Loughs were within easy distance of the place of his captivity, and more suitable for embarkation than any seaport in the West of Ireland if North Britain were his destination.

A voyage from the west coast of Ireland to the Clyde would take the Saint a very unnecessary journey of 200 miles by land to the port of embarkation, and from thence an equally unnecessary voyage by sea, from the west around the northern coast of Ireland, past North Antrim—the county from which he started,—in order to reach Dumbarton, Kilpatrick, or Hamilton on the Clyde.

There are some indications which suggest that St. Patrick, when returning to his native country, sailed from Killala Bay. Although Killala is only 130 miles distant from Mount Slemish, as the crow flies, the Saint would have had to travel around Slieve Gallion, and make a circuit around the mountains of Tyrone, which stood directly across the path of a direct route. Lough Erne, in the County of Fermanagh, and Lough Gill, in the County of Sligo, and the inland flow of Killala Bay would add to the obstacles to be encountered, sufficient when all taken together to account for the 53 miles difference between 130, as the crow flies, and 183 English or 200 Roman miles which had to be travelled before he joined his ship.

Moreover, the woods of Foclut were situated within five miles of Killala, and St. Patrick in his "Confession" speaks in familiar terms of the inhabitants who dwell in the neighbourhood of the woods, whose voices sounded familiar to his ears when far away in Gaul.

This, indeed, would suggest that the Saint had made acquaintance with them during his flight, for he distinctly states when alluding to the place of his embarkation: "I had never been there, nor did I know any one that lived there" ("Confession"). His acquaintance with the inhabitants of Foclut must have been made after he had journeyed there, and previous to his embarkation.

Readers of the "Confession" will remember how touchingly he described the cordial manner in which he was welcomed by his relatives, who, to use the Saint's own words, "received me as a son, and besought me that then at least, after I had undergone so many tribulations, I should never depart from them again. Then in the middle of the night, a man who seemed to come from Ireland, whose name was Victoricus, the bearer of innumerable letters, one of which he handed to me; and I read the beginning of the letter, entitled 'The Voice of the Irish.' As I was reading the beginning of the letter, I thought that I heard in my mind the voices who dwelt near the woods of Foclut, which is near the Western sea, and they cried out: 'We entreat thee, O holy youth, to come and walk still with us.' My heart was deeply touched; I could read no more; and I awoke" ("Confession").

Being then in his thirtieth year when he had this vision, St. Patrick could not be called a youth. He was a youth, however, at the time when he escaped from his first captivity, and became acquainted with the inhabitants of Foclut, who appealed to him in the vision as the youth they had formerly known. They, consequently, besought him to come and abide with them as he had done formerly, for this is the obvious meaning of the words "We entreat thee, O holy youth, to come and walk still with us."

It is probable, therefore, that St. Patrick sailed back from Killala Bay, the nearest port to the woods of Foclut. It may readily be surmised that if the saintly youth, so full of holy zeal, had to remain for a few weeks, or even a few days, whilst the ship was completing its cargo, he would have time to make friendly acquaintance with the inhabitants near the woods, who doubtless received the friendless stranger with kind hospitality.

This gives a simple solution of the difficulty proposed by Professor Bury, who, relying on St. Patrick's friendly acquaintance with the inhabitants of Foclut, states that Croagh Patrick, which is not far from Foclut, and not Mount Slemish, was the scene of the Saint's captivity.

If the ship's cargo consisted chiefly of Irish wolfhounds, so greatly appreciated in Gaul, as Professor Bury suggests (p. 30), it would take more than "a day or two" to collect a sufficient number for exportation. There is nothing stated in the "Confession" to limit the time that St. Patrick had to wait before the ship, sailed away from port.

Moreover, in the solitude of Mount Slemish, absorbed in prayer and in guarding his flock, the saintly shepherd had no opportunity of making any acquaintance whilst in slavery. "After I had come to Ireland I was daily attending sheep, and I frequently prayed during the day, and the love of God and His faith and fear increased in me more and more, and the spirit was stirred; so that in a single day I have said as many as a hundred prayers, and in the night nearly the same, so that

I remained in the woods and on the mountain. Even before the dawn I was roused to prayer in snow, in ice and rain, and I felt no injury from it, nor was there any want of energy in me, as I see now, because the spirit was then fervent in me." These certainly are not the words of a youth who was in the habit of journeying from Croagh Patrick to Foclut to make the acquaintance of the inhabitants. It is, on the contrary, easy to imagine what a powerful effect a Saint, so stirred by the Spirit of God as his words express, would have on all with whom he came in contact after he had been freed from his duties as a shepherd. St. Patrick's history of himself suggests at least that his acquaintance with others, except those of his master's household, must have been made after his escape from captivity.

Professor Bury, however, is the latest convert to the opinion that St. Patrick fled to Gaul, and not to the Island of Britain, after his escape from captivity in Ireland. The Professor narrates that considerable regions in Gaul were a desolate wilderness, according to contemporary rhetorical and poetical evidence, from A.D. 408 to 416, and, therefore, it might be argued, Gaul suits the narrative of St. Patrick in his "Confession." He and his companions reached land three days (*post triduum*) after they left the coast of Ireland, so that our choice lies between Britain and Gaul. The data do not suit Britain. We cannot imagine what inland part of Britain they could have wished to reach which would necessitate a journey of twenty-eight days *per desertum*. Suppose the crew disembarked on the south coast of Britain, and that the southern regions had been recently ravaged by the Saxons, yet a journey of a few days would have brought them to Londinium, or any other place they could have desired to reach from a south port. Moreover, if they had landed in Britain, Patrick, when he once escaped from their company, could have reached his home in a few days, whereas he did not return for a few years. His own words exclude Britain. Having mentioned his final escape from the traders, he proceeds: "iterum post paucos annos in Britanniis eram cum parentibus meis." I believe that "post paucos annos" has been interpreted by some in this sense: "a few years after my capture." But this is an unnatural explanation. The words naturally refer to what immediately precedes, namely, his escape. The only thing that can be alleged in favour of Britain is the intimation in the dream that he would "quickly come to his native land" (*cito iturus ad patriam tuam*). "This, of course," continues the Professor, "represented his expectations at the time of his escape. But the very fact that he fails to say that the promise was literally fulfilled, and glides over the intervening years in silence, strongly suggests that his expectation was not realised" (Appendix C, pp. 339—340).

Professor Bury, being a Protestant, treats the Divine admonition given to the Saint as a dream; not as the voice of God speaking to His servant, but as an ardent desire on the Saint's part which met with disappointment. Catholics, on the contrary, fully believe that God's promise was fulfilled, and that St. Patrick did actually return to his own native country, which the Professor very satisfactorily proves was Gaul and not Britain. The Armorican theory of St. Patrick's birthplace affords a very natural and easy explanation of the difficulty which the Saint's return to Gaul from captivity must present to all who try to prove that he was a native of Great Britain.

# ST. FIACC'S NEMTHUR WAS SITUATED IN THE SUBURBS OF BOULOGNE

## I.

Natus est Patritius Nemturri
Ut refertur in narrationibus,
Juvenis (fuit) sex annorem decem
Quando ductus est sub vinculis.

## II.

Succat ejus notnen in Tribubus dictum,
Quis ejus Pater sit notum,
Filius (fuit) Calpurnii, filii Otidi,
Nepos deaconi Odissi.

## III.

Fuit sex annis in servitate,
Excis hominum (Gentilium) non vescebat,
Fuit ei nomen adoptivum Cothriagh
Quatuor Tribubus quia inserviit.

## IV.

Dixit Victor(ei) servo
Milchonis, Iret trans fluctus.
Posuit suos pedes supra saxum,
Manet exinde ejus vestigia.

## V.

Profectus est trans Alpes omnes,
Trans Maria, fuit faelix expedition
Et remansit apud Germanum
In australi parte australis Lethaniae.

CALIGULA'S TOWER, CALLED NEMTOR BY THE MARINI.

The following beautiful free translation of these verses is taken, with kind permission, from Monsignor Edward Watson, M.A.'s, translation of St. Fiacc's ode:

## I.

"At Nemthur, as our minstrels own,
Heaven's radiance first on Patrick smiled,
But fifteen summers scarce had thrown
A halo round the holy child,
When captured by an Irish band
He took their Isle for fatherland.
Succat by Christian birth his name,
Heir to a noble father's fame.
Calphurnius' son, of Potit's race,
And deacon Odis' kin and grace,
Six years of bondage he must bear
With faithful fast from heathen fare.
And Cothriagh now his name and due,
Who holding high allegiance true,
Yet served four little lords of earth
(God's servant he of forefold worth)
Till Victor bade him Milchu's slave
To fly across the freeman's wave.
He fled, but first upon the rocky shore
His footprint set a seal for evermore.

## II.

Then far away beyond the seas,
In happy flight o'er many a land,
O'er many a mountain on he flees
To face Lethania's southern strand,
Nor rested long upon the road
Until he gained Germain's abode."

St. Fiacc states that the Apostle of Ireland was born at Nemthur—Nemthur, as all commentators agree, is not the name of a town, but of a tower. "Neamthur Hebernica vox est quse coelestem, sive altam turrim denotat." "Neamthur is an Irish word which denotes a heavenly, or a high tower" (Rerum Hibernicarum Scriptores Veteres, Tom i., p. 96—O'Conor).

Assuming that St. Patrick was born in the suburbs, and close to the town of Bononia, or Banaven, as it has already been proved from his "Confession," St. Fiacc's declaration that his Patron was born at Nemthur admits of a very lucid explanation. Nemthur was situated in the suburbs and close to the town of Bonaven. St. Fiacc gives the name of the district, but St. Patrick gives the name of the town near which he was born.

Singularly enough Caligula's famous tower on the sea coast of Boulogne was called Turris Ordinis by the Romans, but Nemtor by the Gauls, as Hersart de la

Villemarque clearly proves in his "Celtic Legend" (p. 213), and the tower itself has given its name to the locality where it once stood, which is called even at the present time Tour d'Ordre—the French translation of "Turris Ordinis."

The history of this tower, on account of its close connection with the history of St. Patrick, cannot fail to be interesting. Caligula, or Caius Caesar, who died A.D. 41, meditated a descent upon Britain, and with that object marshalled his troops at Bononia. Fearful, however, of the dangers and fatigues of a long campaign in that inhospitable island, and full of childish vanity, he determined at length, as Suetonius humorously observes, "to make war in earnest; he drew up his army on the shore of the ocean, with his ballistse and other engines of war, and, while no one could imagine what he intended to do, on a sudden commanded them to gather up sea shells and fill their helmets and the folds of their dresses with them, calling them 'the spoils of the ocean due to the Capitol and the Palatium.' As a monument of his success, he raised a lofty tower, upon which, as at Pharos, he ordered lights to be burnt in the night time for the guidance of ships at sea" ("Lives of the Twelve Caesars," Caligula, p. 283).

"It seems generally agreed," writes Forester, the translator of Suetonius' Lives, "that the point of the coast which was signalised by this ridiculous bravado of Caligula, somewhat redeemed by the erection of a high house, was Itium, afterwards called Gessoriacum and Bononia (Boulogne), a town belonging to the Gaulish tribe of the Morini" (note, p. 283).

For many centuries this tower called Turris Ordens, Turris Ardens, or Turris Ordinis by the Romans, and Neamthur by the Gauls, spread its light over land and sea on the north-eastern cliffs of Boulogne.

A description of the tower is given in the "Memoirs of the Academy of Inscription," quoted by Bertrand in his "History of Boulogne," as follows: "The form of this monument, one of the most striking erected by the Romans, was octagon. It was entirely abolished about a hundred years ago, but, fortunately, a drawing of it, made when the lighthouse was still perfect, is still in existence, and has been exhibited to the Academy by the learned Father Lequien, a Dominican monk, native of Boulogne. Each of its sides, according to Bucherius, measured 24 to 25 feet, so that its circumference was about 200, and its diameter 66 feet. It contained twelve entablatures, or species of galleries, on the outside, including that on the ground floor. Each gallery projected a foot and a half further than the one above it, and consequently their size diminished with each succeeding gallery. On the top fires were lighted to serve as a beacon to vessels at sea. A solid foundation was formed, not only under the lighthouse, but for some distance beyond the external walls. It was constructed of stones and bricks in the following manner: first were seen three layers of stones, found on the coast, of iron grey colour, then two layers of yellow stone of a softer nature, and upon these two rows of hard red bricks, two inches thick, and a foot and a half long, and a little more than a foot broad" ("Bertrand's History of Boulogne," pp. 13, 14).

"Caligula's tower was built on the north-eastern cliffs, about half a mile from the sea, but within the suburbs of Boulogne. The constant encroachment of the tide had reduced that distance to 400 feet in 1544, when Boulogne was captured, and fortifications built around the tower by the English troops. Still, however, the merciless waves rushed onward to the coast, undermining the cliffs more and more, until at length, on July 29th, 1644, Caligula's tower fell headlong with a crash into the sea.

"Passengers from Folkestone to Boulogne gaze with reverence or curiosity on the Calvary on the northeastern cliffs, which fishermen salute with uncovered heads when sailing out to reap the harvest of the sea. Close to the Calvary there is a mass of ruins overhanging the cliff, which is all that remains of the fortifications built round Caligula's tower by the English conquerors. The tower itself once stood over the site occupied by the Hotel du Pavillion et des Bains de Mer, opposite the place for sea bathing" ("Bertrand's History of Boulogne," pp. 15, 16).

"The Celtic Legend," published by Hersart de la Villemarque in 1864, clearly shows how the history of Bononia and of its celebrated tower is connected with his—St. Patrick's—life. One of the legends is entitled "St. Patrick," and commences as follows: "On the shore of the channel separating England from France, near the famous place from which Caesar embarked for the Isles of Britain, a fortified enclosure was erected overlooking and protecting the coast and territory which formed part of the possession of the Morini Gauls. This important strategic point was called in Latin, Tabernia, or the 'Field of Tents' (Le Champs du Pavilion), because the Roman army had pitched their tents there. About a mile distant, a group of buildings formed a fairly-sized village, which at first was called by the Gauls Gessoriac, *then Bonauen Armorik*, and afterwards named Bononia Oceasensis by the Roman Gauls, and finally Boulogne-sur-Mer by the French.

"A light-house, or Nemtor, as it was called in the Celtic language, kept watch during the night over the camp, village, and sea, preserving the Gaulish frontier from piratical incursions.

"At the foot of the light-house stood the residence of a Roman officer named Calphurnius, who had the supervision of the fire in the tower, amongst the more costly and ornamented houses than the others, where the free-and-easy life and customs of the Romans found a last refuge. He lived there attended by domestic and military servants. He had fought under the Imperial flag and attained the rank of a Decurion (p. 354). . . .

"Forgetfulness of God, disobedience to His laws, which are also the best laws of human society, led to the ruin both of the colony of Bononia and of St. Patrick's family. One day a mutiny, from which the servants of Calphurnius could not have kept aloof, broke out amongst the soldiers in the camp, just at the time when pirates, who had come from different parts of the Irish coast and formed themselves into a fleet so as to plunder the towns on the sea coast of Gaul with greater security, took advantage of the dissensions amongst the inhabitants of Boulogne and besieged the town. Fine furniture, carpets, and valuable garments, vessels of gold and silver, arms and instruments of every kind, everything that they could seize in the houses, in the town, in the camp, in the rural dwellings close by, in the stables, in the ox stalls, in the sheep pens: horses, cows, pigs, cattle and sheep were carried off and placed on board the ships. Those who attempted any resistance were put to death, whilst others, undergoing the fate of domestic animals, were sold into slavery. Amongst the defenders of the colony who perished were Calphurnius, his wife, and many of his household. St. Patrick was numbered amongst the captives. The corsairs, having set sail, landed him in Ireland, where they sold him to a small chieftain in Ulster named Milcho" ("La Legende Celtique," par le Vicomte Hersart de la Villemarque, Membre de l'Institut Paris, 1864, Librarie Academique. Dedier et Cie., Librarie Editeurs, 35 Quai des Augustines).

There is a constant tradition that St. Patrick was a native of Boulogne, and that tradition is expressed in the Celtic Legend just quoted. Even the present "Guide Book" of that town (Merridew's, 1905) volunteers the following information, which, although erroneous as to dates, is interesting as referring to St. Patrick's connection with the city: "About the year 249 St. Patrick arrived in Morinia, and for some time resided at Boulogne" (p. 10). Feather Malbrancq, in his "History of the Morini," quotes the "Chronicon Morinense," "The Life of St. Arnulphus," and "The Catalogue of the Bishops of that See" to prove St. Patrick's connection with the town. Although it is certain that St. Patrick never presided over that See, the fact of his being numbered amongst the Bishops admits of an easy explanation if he was a native of that town.

# ST. FIACC DESCRIBES ST. PATRICK'S FLIGHT FROM IRELAND TO ARMORICA

ST. FIACC poetically describes St. Patrick's flight to his-own native country in the fifth stanza of his hymn:

"Then far away beyond the seas,
In happy flight o'er many a land,
O'er many a mountain on he flees
To fair Lethania's Southern strand,
Nor rested long upon the road
Until he gained Germain's abode."

It is evident from this that St. Patrick fled direct to Lethania after his escape from captivity in Ireland, having received the angel's promise that he should return to his native land. O'Conor testifies that the Irish called not only Armorica, Lethania, but all Western Gaul as far as the Diocese of Auxerre. ("Lethaniam appellabant Hiberni non modo Armoricam sed et occidentalem Galliam usque ad diocesim Antisiodorensem") ("Rerum Hibernicarum Scriptores Veteres Tom," L, p. 91, note).

# THE SCHOLIAST PRACTICALLY ADMITS ST. PATRICK'S BIRTH IN ARMORICA

THE Scholiast, who annotated St. Fiacc's "Metrical Life of St. Patrick," flourished in the eleventh century, according to Professor Bury. The scholia of the Scholiast, however, should be received with great caution, as Lanigan points out: "The scholia of the Scholiast," he remarks, "are not the composition of one person. For instance, in scholion 5, the Letha mentioned in the hymn is properly explained by Armorica, or the maritime tract on the North-West of Gaul; while in scholion n it is interpreted of Latium, in Italy. In scholion 9 we read that on a certain occasion St. Patrick said, 'Dar mo dhe broth,' which is explained, 'God is able to do this if He choose'; and yet immediately after it is added that 'Dar mo dhe broth' was a sort of asseveration familiar to St. Patrick, signifying 'By my God, Judge, or judgment.' On the whole, it is evident that the scholia, as we have them at present, are a compilation of observations, some more, some less ancient, extracted from various writers" ("Eccl. Hist, of Ireland," vol. L, c. iii., p. 81).

The scholion (i) on St. Fiacc's opening words: "Natus est Patritius Nemturri"—"St. Patrick was born at Nemthur"—is as follows: "Nemthur is a city in the Northern parts of Britain, viz. Alcluid (nempe Alcluida)." By comparing this scholion with the scholion given later on (c. iii.), it will be seen that the same pen has not written both scholia. The scholion referred to is this: "The cause of St. Patrick's captivity was this: His father, Calphurnius, and his mother, Conchessa, and his five sisters, Lupita, Tigris, Liemania, and Darerca, Cinnena was the name of the fifth, and his brother deacon, Senanus, all together travelled from Britain Alcluid southwards over the Sea of Ictium to Armorican Lethania, or Britannia Lethania, both on business and because a certain relative of theirs dwelt there, and the mother of the above-named children, namely Conchessa, was of the Franks, and a near relative of St. Martin. At that time, however, seven sons of Fachmad, King of the Britons, broke loose from Britain and plundered Armorican Britain in the territory of Letha, where St. Patrick happened to be living with his family. They slew Calphurnius there, and carried off St. Patrick and his sister Lupita captives to Ireland. They sold Lupita 'in Connallia Murthemnensi' [a territory in Ulster], and Patrick in the northern parts of the territory of the Dal-aradia."

The contradictory nature of the accounts given by the Scholiast as to St. Patrick's supposed birth in Alcluid, or Dumbarton, and his capture in Armorica will be seen by comparing them with the statement made by the Saint himself in his "Confession": "I, Patrick, a sinner and the most uncultured and humblest of all the faithful, had a father named Calphurnius, a deacon, the son of Potitus, a priest, who hailed from the suburban district of Bonaven Taberniae, for he possessed a little country seat close by from whence I was led captive." This statement of the Saint disproves the assertion of the Scholiast that Calphurnius and his family were on a friendly visit to Armorica when all the calamities befell them, for the Saint distinctly states that his father hailed from Bonaven Taberniae, and that he himself was actually residing at his father's little country seat in the suburbs of that town at the time when he was forced into captivity.

It is evident, therefore, from the Scholiast that Bonaven Tabernise was situated in Armorican Britain; and from St. Patrick's "Confession," that the town from which he was led captive was his own native town. The Apostle of Ireland could not, therefore, as the Scholiast suggests, have been born at Alcluid, or Dumbarton. It is curious to observe how unconsciously the Scholiast connects Calphurnius and his family with Boulogne. Calphurnius and his family are made to sail from Dumbarton, over the Sea of Itius or Ictius, to Armorica. Hersart de la Villemarque has already identified Bonaven under its various names as Bononia or Boulogne. It was called Itius or Ictius by Caesar, Bononia by the Romans, and Bonauen Armorik by the Gaulish Celts. The Scholiast, therefore, when he directs the course of Calphurnius and his family across the Sea of Ictius, seems to be steering their ship directly to Boulogne.

Nemthur cannot possibly be the name of the town near which St. Patrick was born, simply because the Saint gives the name of Bonaven, or Bononia, as the city of his birth. St. Fiacc does not name Nemthur as a town; he simply tells us that St. Patrick was born at Nemthur, which, as has been proved, was both the name of the Caligula's tower and of the district in which that tower stood in the suburbs of Bonaven. The Scholiast is the first to call Nemthur a town, and evidently puts it down as the ancient name of Alcluid, or Dumbarton. This is the obvious meaning of the scholion: "Nemthur est civitas in septentrional! Britanni nempe Alcluida." Nemthur is a city in northern Britain, namely Alcluid. The "nempe Alcluida" looks very much like an interpolation, and if an interpolation, the statement of the Scholiast that Nemthur is a city in northern Britain, without the addition "nempe Alcluida," might easily refer to Northern Britain in Gaul where, however, Nemthur was not the name of a city, but the name both of a tower and of the district of the city where St. Patrick was born.

Neither the Scholiast, nor those who have adopted his views as to the Saint's birth at Dumbarton, have ever answered Lanigan's challenge, who boldly states that the name Nemthur is not to be found in Nennius's "List of British Towns," which Usher himself had illustrated, nor in any of the old "Itineraries," or in Ricardus Corinensis, or in Camden, or Horsley &c. (vol. i, b. 3, p. 91).

The learned Cardinal Moran, in the March of the *Dublin Review*, 1880, endeavoured to take up the gauntlet and answer Lanigan's challenge by quoting one of Taliessin's poems from the "Black Book of Carmarthen," which represents a Welsh hero sailing away with an army to Scotland and recovering his lost inheritance in a battle fought and won at Nevthur in Clydesdale.

Besides the fact that no small stretch of imagination is required to believe that

Nevthur and Nemthur are one and the same, nearly all the poems attributed to Taliessin are regarded as spurious by learned critics, as Chamber's "Encyclopaedia," under the heading Welsh Literature, evidently points out.

"Mr. Nash, the author of 'Taliessin and the Bards and Druids of Wales,' enables us to form an independent judgment on this point, for he translates some fifty of the poems, and we find that, instead of their exhibiting an antique Welsh character, they abound in allusions to mediaeval theology, and frequently employ mediaeval Latin terms. It is certainly unfortunate for the reputation of the 'Chief of Bards' that the specimens of his poems, which are considered genuine, possess exceedingly small merit. The life of this famous but over-rated genius is, of course, enveloped in legend." Lanigan's challenge, therefore, still remains unanswered, and a town mamed Nemthur is not to be found in any ancient history, geography, or map. The error, therefore, of the Scholiast consisted in stating that Alcluid and Nemthur were identical, but his statement that St. Patrick was captured in Armorica is historically true.

# THE "TREPARTITE LIFE" FALLS INTO THE SAME ERROR

THE following account is given in the "Trepartite Life" concerning St. Patrick's native town, and the country from which he was taken captive: —

"Patrick, then, was of the Britons of Alcluid by origin. Calphurn was his father's name. He was a noble priest. Potit was his grandfather's name, whose title was a deacon. Conceis was his mother's name. She was of the Franks, and a sister to St. Martin. In Nemthur, moreover, was the man Patrick born. . . .

"The cause of Patrick's coming to Erin was as follows: 'The seven sons of Fachmad, namely—the seven sons of the King of Britain—were on a naval expedition, and they went to plunder Armoric Letha; and a number of Britons of Strath-Cluaidh were on a visit with their kinsmen—the Britons of Armoric Letha—and Calphurn, son of Potit, Patrick's father, and her mother Conceis, daughter of Ocbas of the Gauls, that is of the Franks, were killed in the slaughter in Armorica. Patrick and his two sisters, viz. Lupait and Tigris, were taken prisoners, moreover, in that slaughter. The seven sons of Fachmad went afterwards to sea, having with them Patrick and his two sisters in captivity. The way they went was around Erin, northwards, until they landed in the north, and they sold Patrick to Miluic, son of Baun, that is, the King of Dal-Araidhe.

"They sold his two sisters in Conaille Muirthemne. And they did not know this. Four persons, truly, that purchased him. One of them was Miluic. It was from this that he received the name Cothriage, for the reasons that he served four masters. He had, indeed, four names" (W. M. Hennessey's Translation of the "Trepartite Life").

The author of the "Trepartite Life" repeats the contradictory statements of the Scholiast, namely, that St. Patrick was born at Dumbarton and captured in Armorica, and it stands refuted by St. Patrick himsel in his "Confession," who declares that his father hailed from Bonaven, where the Roman encampment stood, and that he himself was captured whilst residing at his father's villula, or country seat, close by the town. Just as we are bound to credit St. Patrick's "Confession;" the statements of the Scholiast, and of the author of the "Trepartite Life," that he was simply on a visit to his relatives in Armorica when captured, must be discredited.

Ignoring the fact that the author of the "Tripartite Life" and Probus tell the same tale, the Archbishop of Tuam, in his excellent "Life of St. Patrick," states "that the Scholiast on St. Fiacc whilst expressly declaring that Nemthur, St. Patrick's birthplace, was in North Britain, namely, Ail Cluade, adds that young Patrick, with his parents, brother and sisters, went from the Britons of Ail Cluade over the Ictian Sea, southwards, to visit his relatives in Armorica, and that it was from Latevian Armorica that Patrick was carried off captive to Ireland. The Scholiast here confounds the Armoric Britons of the Clyde with the Armoric Britons of Gaul, or Letavia, who had no existence then at so early a date. No doubt they were kindred Britons, but the name Britannia and Britons were not at that time given to Armorica of Gaul" (Appendix i., p. 585).

Nothing is here said by His Grace about Probus or the "Tripartite Life," who agree with the Scholiast that the Saint was captured in Armorica. When treating of Britannia in Gaul, it will be proved from the "Sacred Histories of Sulpicius Severus" that Armorica was called Britannia when the Council of Ariminium was held in the year 359. It is evident, however, that the author of the "Tripartite Life" was firmly convinced that St. Patrick was captured in Armorica, from the description he gives of the flight of his captors: "The seven sons of Fachmad went afterwards on the sea, having with them Patrick and his two sisters in captivity. The way they went was northward around Erin, until they landed in the north, and they sold Patrick to Miluic."

From this narrative it is evident that the captives were carried by the fleet northwards around Erin until they arrived in the neighbourhood of Lough Larne, Antrim, where St. Patrick was sold as a slave. The captors afterwards sailed southwards and sold St. Patrick's sisters at Louth. They must, therefore, as Father Bullen Morris surmises, have sailed around the western coast of Erin after sailing away from Armorica. It is clear, as the same writer does not fail to observe, that such a course cannot fit in with the Dumbarton theory: "A voyage northwards from the mouth of the Clyde would take the Irish fleet to the North Pole" ("Ireland and St. Patrick," p. 26).

The Scholiast and the author of the "Tripartite Life" are of opinion that St. Patrick was made captive by the seven sons of Fachmad, King of Britain, who are represented as making a raid into Armorica. Jocelin declares that the capture was made by pirates. The Second, Third, and Fourth "Lives" are unanimous in stating that the Saint was captured by the Irish Scots. St. Patrick's own words in the Epistle to Coroticus, "Have I not tender mercy on that nation which formerly took me captive?" leave no doubt as to his capture by the Irish Scots. Colgan endeavours to harmonise both accounts by suggesting that the sons of Fachmad were British exiles in Ireland, who fought under the standard of King Niall when he invaded Armorica, and that they may have been the actual captors of the Saint.

# ALL THAT THE SECOND
# AND THIRD "LIVES" TESTIFY

As the Second and Third "Lives of St. Patrick" are practically and almost verbally identical up to the end of Section XL, the same translation up to that point will suffice for both.

"Patrick was born at Nemthur. He had a sister named Lupita, whose relics are preserved at Armagh. Patrick was born in the Field of Tents. It was called Campus Tabernaculorum because the Roman army, at some time or other, pitched their tents there during the cold winter season.

"IV.—The boy, however, was reared at Nemthur. . . .

"XI.—This was the cause of his exile and arrival in Ireland: An army of Irish Scots embarked, as usual, in their ships, and forming a large fleet sailed over to Britain, and brought back from thence many captives and carried them to Ireland, the captives numbering altogether one hundred of both sexes. Patrick was, as he himself testifies, in his sixteenth year at that time."

The following addition is given in the Third "Life": "Patrick, who was also called Suchet, was sprung from the British nation, and his country and the place where he was born was situated not far from the sea. His father's name was 'Calburnius,' the son of a venerable man named Potitus; but his mother, Conches by name, was the daughter of Dechusius. Both parents of this holy man were devoted to religion."

Controversially speaking, neither of these two "Lives" are of any value. Nemthur is not identified with Dumbarton, and it is not clearly stated whether the Irish fleet raided the island of Britain or Armorican Britain, or whether St. Patrick was descended from the Island or Armorican Britons. A recent writer lays much stress on the fact that the British word Tabern is used to denote a tent field in the Second, Third, and Fourth "Lives," but the argument does not carry with it much weight, for according to Camden the British and Gaulish Celts spoke the same language, so that it is just as favourable to Armorica as to the island of Britain (" Britannia," vol. i., p. 11).

# THE FOURTH "LIFE"

"SOME say that St. Patrick was of Jewish origin. After Our Lord had died on the Cross for the sins of the human race, a Roman army, avenging His Passion, laid Judea waste, and the captive Jews were dispersed amongst all the nations of the earth. Some of their number settled down among the Armorican Britons, and it is stated that it was from them that St. Patrick traced his origin." This may be gathered from the book of Epistles composed by himself, "on account of our sins, and because we had neither observed the precepts of the Lord nor obeyed His Commandments, we are dispersed to the uttermost ends of the earth."

"But, however, it is more credible and more certain that he speaks of that dispersion into which the Britons were driven by the Romans, in order that they might become possessed of the land near the Tuscan Sea which is called Armorica. After that dispersion, therefore, his parents went straight to Strath Clyde. There St. Patrick was conceived and born, his father being 'Kalburnius,' and his mother Conchessa, as he testifies in the book of his Epistles: 'I am Patrick, the son of Kalburnius, and Conchessa is my mother.' St. Patrick was, therefore, born in a town called Nemthur, which signifies a heavenly tower. This town was situated in Campo Tabernise, which is called the Field of Tents because, at one time, the Roman army pitched their tents there. In the British tongue Campus Tabern is the same as Campus Tabernaculorum.

"XV.—But the first cause of his coming to Ireland, and the sequence of events which hurried him there, are not to be passed over in silence. By the divine providence of God, it so happened that in his tender years he should be led to that nation, so that in his youth he should learn the language of the people, whose apostle he was afterwards destined to become. At that period Irish fleets were accustomed to sail over to Britain for the sake of plunder, and to bring back to Ireland whomsoever they made prisoners. It chanced, therefore, that the venerated youth, with his sister, named Lupita, should be taken captives amongst others. Some have written that the Saint at the time was but seven years of age. It seems to me, however, more credible what he himself states: 'When I fell into captivity I was sixteen years of age.' He was taken to Ireland and sold in the northern regions to four brothers, whom he served with a simple and devout heart. On that account he was called Cothraigh. But he had four names, for he received the name of Suchet at baptism; he was called Magonius by Germanus, Bishop; lastly, when he was elevated to the Episcopal dignity, he received his fourth name, Patrick."

It is suggestive how the Armorican tradition seems to manifest itself, either directly or indirectly, in nearly all the "Lives" of the Saint which are considered the best; in St. Fiacc's, in the annotations of the Scholiast, in the "Tripartite Life," in the Fourth "Life," and in the Fifth by Probus. In the Fourth "Life" it is stated that both parents of the Saint were Armorican Britons, and that St. Patrick, except for the accident of his place of birth, was an Armorican Briton. The author of the Fourth "Life," moreover, calls Calphurnius and Conchessa Armorican Britons, which serves to demonstrate that Armorica, even in the early years of St. Patrick, fell under the name of Britannia, and that its inhabitants were called Britons.

In this "Life" is to be found the mistake of the Scholiast, and of the other "Lives" who have adopted his suggestion, that Nemthur was the name of a town, and not of a tower or district, as may be gathered from the history of the tower itself.

The Second, Third, and Fourth "Lives" of the Saint, however, "are filled with fables," according to Canon O'Hanlon. "Their acts seem to have been either borrowed from one another, or are copies of versions taken from the same source" ("Lives of the Irish Saints," March 17th).

# THE SIXTH "LIFE OF ST. PATRICK," BY JOCELIN

"THERE was a man named Calphurnius, the son of Potitus, a presbyter, by nation a Briton, living in the village Taburnia (that is the Field of Tents), near the town of Empthor, and his habitation was nigh unto the Irish Sea. This man married a French damsel named Concuessa, niece of the blessed Martin, Archbishop of Tours, and the damsel was elegant in her form and in her manners, for, having been brought from France with her elder sister into the northern parts of Britain, they were sold at the command of her father. Calphurnius being pleased with her manners, charmed with her attentions, and attracted by her beauty, very much loved her, and from the state of serving maid in his household, raised her to be his companion in wedlock. And her sister, having been delivered unto another man, lived in the aforementioned town of Empthor.

"And Calphurnius and his wife were just before God, walking without offence in the justifications of the Lord, and they were eminent in their birth, and in their faith, and in their hope, and in their religion. And though in their outward habit and abiding they seemed to serve under the yoke of Babylon, yet did they in their acts and in their conversation show themselves citizens of Jerusalem. Therefore out of the earth of their flesh, being freed from the tares of sin and from the noxious weeds of vice by the ploughshare of evangelic and apostolic learning, and being fruitful in the growth of all virtues, did they, as the best and richest fruit, bring forth a son, whom, when he had at the font put off the old man, they caused to be named Patritius, as being the future father and patron of many nations; of whom, even at his baptism, the God that is Three in One was pleased by the sign of a threefold miracle to declare how pure a vessel of election should he prove, and how devoted a worshipper of the Holy Trinity. But after a little while, this happy birth being completed, they vowed themselves by mutual consent unto chastity, and with a holy end rested in the Lord. But Calphurnius-first served God a long time in the deaconship, and at length closed his days in the priesthood. . . ."

Chapter XII.—"As, according to the testimony of Holy Writ, the furnace tries the gold, so did the hour of trial draw near to Patrick that he might the more provedly receive the crown of life. For when the illustrious boy had perlustrated three lustres, already attaining his sixteenth year, he was, with many of his-fellow-countrymen, seized by the pirates who were ravaging the borders, and was made captive and carried into Ireland, and was there sold as a slave to a certain pagan prince named Milcho, who reigned in the Northern parts of the island, even at the same age when Joseph is recorded to have been sold in Egypt. . . ."

Chapter XVII.—"And St. Patrick, guided by his angelic guide, came to the sea, and he there found a ship that was to carry him to Britain, and a crew of heathens, who were in the ship, freely received him, and hoisting their sails with a favourable wind, after three days they made land. And, being come out of the ship, they found a region deserted and inhabited by none, and they began to travel over the whole country for the space of twenty-eight days; and for want of food in that fearful and wild solitude were they perishing of hunger" (Jocelin's "Life of St. Patrick," translated by E. L. Swift).

Jocelin's "Life of St. Patrick" deserves the harsh sentence pronounced upon it by Canon O'Hanlon: "It is incomparably the worst" of all the Latin "Lives" of the Saint. Jocelin represents Conchessa, St. Patrick's saintly mother, as a niece of St. Martin of Tours, and, almost in the same breath, suggests that either St. Martin's brother, or his brother-in-law, sold Conchessa and her elder sister to Calphurnius, a Briton of Clydesdale, as slaves. Although Conchessa was sold as a slave "at the command of her father," she is said to have succeeded in captivating and marrying her master Calphurnius.

Whilst Ware and Usher sneer at Jocelin's statement that Calphurnius and Conchessa took the vow of celibacy and devoted themselves to a religious life immediately after St. Patrick's birth, they eagerly adopt Jocelin's statement that the Apostle of Ireland was born at "Empthor," and that the home of The Sixth "Life," Calphurnius was "not far from the Irish Sea," although this untrustworthy author stands alone among the ancient writers in making this assertion.

Although Jocelin is responsible for the statement that St. Patrick fled to the island of Britain after his escape from captivity in Ireland, the subsequent three days' voyage by sea and twenty-eight days' journey by land before reaching his home are fatal to Jocelin's contention, as Professor Bury clearly demonstrates.

Ware's Empthor was near Dumbarton; Colgan's, Dumbarton itself; Usher and the "Aberdeen Breviary" identify it as Kilpatrick; Cardinal Moran rests sure that it is Hamilton, at the mouth of the Avon in Scotland; but St. Patrick's ship, chartered by Heaven to carry him to his "own native land," could, if any of the places named were St. Patrick's native town, have borne him directly almost to his destination, and saved part at least of the three days' journey by sea and the whole of the twenty-eight days' journey by wilderness before joining his relatives.

# THE FIFTH "LIFE," BY PROBUS, PROVES THAT ST. PATRICK WAS BORN IN BONONIA

THE Fifth "Life," written by Probus, an Irish monk, who died at Meyence in the year 859, is regarded as the best of the old Latin "Lives" of St. Patrick; it is considered to be an amended edition of the "Book of Armagh," written by Muirchu Macc-Mactheni, so truly that the blank left by the missing folio in that famous book can be filled in by copying the "History of Probus." (Canon O'Hanlon's "Lives of the Irish Saints," March 17th.)

The "Life of St. Patrick," by Probus, commences as follows:—

"Cap. I.—St. Patrick, who was also called Suchet, was a Briton by nationality. . . . He was born in Britain [in Britanniis], being the son of Calphurnius, a deacon, who was the son of Potitus, a priest, and his mother was named Conchessa, in a district within the region of Bannaue Tiburniae, not far from the Western Sea, which district, as we have discovered beyond doubt, was situated in the province of Nentria, where the giants are said to have formerly dwelt."

"XII.—When he was in his own country with his father Calphurnius and his mother Conchessa, in their own seaside city [city Arimuric] there was a great outbreak of hostilities in these parts. The sons of King Rithmit, coming from Britain, laid Arimuric and the surrounding country waste. They massacred Calphurnius and his wife Conchessa; but their children, Patrick and his brother Ruchti, together with their sister Mila, they took captives to Ireland. They sold Patrick to Prince Milcho, but his brother Ruchti and his sister Mila to another Prince."

Colgan, in his annotations, substitutes Neutria for Nentria (4), and Armorica for Arimuric, Caesar testifies that all the towus on the sea coast of Armorica were called Armoricse (Britannia, vol i. p. 13). "In his own city Armuric" has therefore been rendered "in his own seaside city."

When Probus wrote his history there was no province in existence called either Nentria or Neutria; but there was a province called Neustria, which embraced Armorica or the northern sea coast of Gaul, where St. Patrick was residing in his own native country (in patria) with his parents, when he was made captive. It follows, likewise, that St. Patrick's native town, "Bannaue Tiburnise," according to Probus, was the seaside city in Armorica referred to. The Bannaue Tiburniae of Probus and the Bonaven Taberniae of St. Patrick are evidently one and the same as Bononia, where the Romans were encamped, which, as it has already been proved, was called Bonauen Armorik by the Gaulish Celts.

If any other proof were needed, the description of the province given by Probus as the country formerly inhabited by giants can leave no doubt on the subject.

Sammes, in his "Antiquities of Ancient Britain," published in 1676, narrates that the Scythians, or Cymri, were called the offspring of Magog by Josephus. Pouring out in mighty hordes from Scythia, they sacked Rome and plundered the Temple of Apollo in Greece. Some of them settled down in Sarmatia, Germany, and Northern Gaul, generally adopting the name of the lands in which they settled. Strabo is quoted as saying "that the very youths (of the Cymri) were half a foot taller than the tallest men," and Manlius for declaring "that the Cymri were a race so exceedingly tall that other nations seemed nothing in their eyes." The same authority narrates that "when one of the Cymri stood in the ranks he seemed of the same proportion as the others, but when he stepped out a few paces, and came near to the Romans, they all began to be amazed at the sight." On that account the Roman soldiers, as Caesar admits, were filled with consternation at the giants they were called upon to encounter when he marched against their leader, Ariovistus. The Cymri were also remarkable for their exceeding swiftness. Csesar witnessed that they "could lay their hands on the manes of horses and keep pace with them in the race." Tully testifies that it was "their joy and delight to die on the battlefield, and that nothing so tormented them as to die idly in their beds." "No wonder," says Sammes, "that they conquered many nations; distressed the Romans themselves, and were a constant thorn in the side of the Gauls" ("Antiquities of Ancient Britain," cap. 2).

Dr. Smith, in his "History of France," narrates that the Cymri "acquired permanent possession of an extensive territory north of the Loire, including the peninsula of Armorica" (p. 13). Bononia, or Boulogne, St. Patrick's native town, was, therefore, situated in Belgic Gaul during the days of Julius Caesar; but, later on, when the descendants of the Cymri, the Belgic Gauls, were almost annihilated in their fierce contests with the Romans, the same province came to be called Armorica. Sulpicius Severus, as we shall see presently, named the same country Britannia at the time of the Council of Ariminium in the year 359—just fourteen years before St. Patrick was born.

In the year 597 Armorica, or Britannia, became absorbed in the province of Neustria, when the kingdom of the Franks was sub-divided into three separate kingdoms, as Dr. Smith relates: "Sigebert became King of Austrasia (in the Prankish tongue, Oster-rike), or the kingdom of the Eastern Franks; Chilperic was recognised as King Neustria (Ne-oster-rike), the land of the Western Franks. The limits of the two kingdoms are somewhat uncertain; but the river Meuse and the Forest of Ardennes may be taken generally as the line of demarcation. Austrasia extended from the Meuse to the Rhine; Neustria extended from the Meuse to the ocean. Gouthran ruled over the division of Gaul which now acquired the name of Burgundy" ("History of France," p. 42).

Neustria, extending from the Meuse to the ocean, necessarily embraced the whole province of Britannia, or Armorica. That province still retained the name of Neustria when Probus, in the tenth century, wrote the "History of St. Patrick."

The change of the name Armorica to Britannia, and from Britannia to Neustria, together with the fact that the name Britannia, or Brittany, as applied to that particular province in Gaul was forgotten for centuries before any of the old Latin "Lives" of St. Patrick, except the first, were written, must have induced some old biographers of the Saint to interpret the name Britain, mentioned in the "Lives" and in the "Confession," as referring only to the Island of Britain,

With the exception of Probus, who had travelled abroad, the old biographers of St. Patrick, on account of their very limited sources of information, had very little knowledge of the histories of foreign countries, and it is not surprising to find them erroneously supposing that St. Patrick was born in Great Britain, because he mentioned in his "Confession" that he was born in Britain, and had relatives among the Britons.

St. Patrick, according to Probus, was one of the Gaulish Britons, being born at Bonaven, or Boulogne-sur-Mer. Although the Saint, according to Canon O'Hanlon, was a little man, he was descended from a race of giants—the bold Cymri, or Celts. That fact established a relationship of race between the Saint and the nation which he converted.

Camden and Keating narrate that King Milesius and his bold Scots, who successfully invaded Ireland, were descended from the Cymri; and it is remarkable that a fierce battle was fought between the Irish Scots and the Tautha de Danans at Mount Slemish, not far from Tralee, in Kerry, which is identical in name with Mount Slemish, in Antrim—the scene of the Saint's captivity ("Britannia," vol. ii., p. 123; "History of Ireland," vol. i., p. 123).

Eochaid O'Flin, a poet quoted by Keating, has left a record of this historical battle:

> "The stout Gadalians first the courage try
> At Sliabh-mis, and rout the enemy:
> Where heroes pierced with many a deadly wound,
> Choked in their blood, lay gasping on the ground:
> Heroes whose brave exploits may justly claim
> Triumphant laurels and immortal fame."

Scota, the relict of King Milesius and mother of Heber and Heremon, Kings of Ireland, was slain while fighting in this battle, and buried in the valley at the foot of Mount Sleabh-mis, which after her interment was called Glean Scoithin, or the Valley of Scota. From her the Irish Scots derived their name. The same old bard has sung a lamentation over her grave:—

> "Beneath, the vale its bosom doth display,
> With meadows green, with flowers profusely gay,
> Where Scota lies, unfortunately slain,
> And with her royal tomb gives honour to the plain.
> Mixed with the first the fair virago fought,
> Sustained the toil of arms and danger sought:

From her the fruitful valley hath the name
O Glean Scoith, and we may trust to fame."

# ST. PATRICK'S FLIGHT TO MARMOUTIER DESCRIBED BY PROBUS

IN the XIVth section of the "Vita Quinta" Probus narrates St. Patrick's arrival in Brotgalum, then his journey to Trajectus, from whence he hastened to Marmoutier to join St. Martin, Bishop of Tours, with whom he remained for four years. Colgan, in his annotations (14), identifies Brotgalum as Burdigalum, or Bordeaux. So, too, does Professor Bury, who tells us that Brodgal was the Irish for Bordeaux, and that "Bordeaux was a regular port for travellers from Ireland to South Gaul" ("Life of St. Patrick," Appendix, p. 341).

Trajectus, according to the old maps, was situated on the river Dordogne, about sixty miles from Tours. From Trajectus St. Patrick had to walk a distance of about two hundred miles through a desert before reaching Tours.

"A glance at the map of ancient Gaul," writes Father Bullen Morris, "will show that in St. Patrick's time a great part of the country between Trajectus and Tours well deserved the name of a desert. The network of rivers, tributaries of the Loire, and now known as La Vienne, La Claire, La Gartempe, &c., must have exposed the country to periodical inundations in those days. So from Tours in the north to Limonum, Alerea, and Legora in the south, east and west, we find some 5,000 square miles, which, as far as the ancient map is concerned, give no signs of possession by man. Travellers entangled amidst these rivers and morasses must have advanced very slowly, and thus it appears that both places and time fit in with St. Patrick's narrative. Nature has changed her face along the line of St. Patrick's journey, and there is little now to remind us of its primeval desolation, save that the rivers still preserve some of their old habits, and now and then combine with the inundations of the giant Loire in setting man at defiance.

"Time, however, with its alternative gifts and ravages, has left untouched the traditions regarding St. Patrick's journey. There is something more than antiquarian interest in the feelings of the Christian traveller who visits the spot on the banks of the Loire, where immemorial tradition and an ancient monument mark the place at which the Saint crossed the river on his way to Marmoutier. At about twenty miles from Tours the railway between that city and Angers stops at the station of St. Patrice; the commune is also named after the Saint, and, as we shall see, there is historical evidence that it has been thus designated for at least nine hundred years."

"The first witness whose evidence we shall take on the subject of the Saint's arrival at St. Patrice is one which many believe to have survived since his time, but on this point the reader must form his own opinion. Above the station, on the side of the hill which rises from the banks of the Loire, we find the famous tree which bears 'the flowers of St. Patrice.' For ages past it has been an object of religious veneration with the people of Touraine, and now in our time it is particularly interesting to find that this devotion was shared by that eminent servant of God, Leon Dupont, the Thaumaturgus of Tours. Monsignor C. Chevalier, President of the Archaeological Society, has published a very full account of the tree and of the traditions connected with it, the subtance of which we subjoin, together with the result of personal investigations made on the spot in August, 1881. At this season the tree was covered with foliage so luxuriant, from the ground upwards, that it was impossible to distinguish the stem, and in every respect it presented the appearance of a tree in its prime, without a sign of decay. It belongs to the botanical class Prunus Spinosa, or blackthorn, and it was covered with berries at the time of our visit. These, however, were the evidence of a second efflorescence in the spring. The celebrity of the tree arises from the fact that every year at Christmas time it is seen covered with flowers, and the tradition at St. Patrice, handed down from father to son, affirms that for fifteen hundred years this phenomenon has been repeated at the same sacred season. It matters not how intense the cold of any particular winter; while the ground beneath and the country around lie covered in their white shroud, the "flowers of St. Patrice" unfold their blossoms and bid defiance to the fierce north winds which sweep the valley of the Loire."

The next witness is the old parish church, dedicated to St. Patrick, which stands about thirty yards from the tree. Its old charters and records show that it dates back from the beginning of the tenth century. One old charter, bearing the date of 1035, contains a deed of gift of some lands adjoining the church of St. Patrick. The church stood on the Roman road between Anjou and Tours. "Thus," concludes Father Bullen Morris, "ancient records and immemorial traditions complete our story, and set St. Patrick on the high road to St. Martin at Marmoutier" ("Ireland and St. Patrick," pp. 35—40).

# BRITAIN IN GAUL
# ST. PATRICK'S NATIVE COUNTRY

UNLESS it can be proved that there was a province called Britain in Gaul, and another Britain quite distinct from the Island of Britain, it would be useless to argue that St. Patrick was a native of Gaul. The Saint represents himself as a native of Britain; and even Probus, who is credited with believing that St. Patrick was a native of Armoric Gaul, distinctly states that the Saint was born in Britain (natus in Britanniis). It is, however, not difficult to prove that there was a province in Gaul called Britain (Britannia) even before the birth of St. Patrick.

Strabo, in his "Description of Europe," narrates in the Fourth Book that about 220 years before Christ, Publius Cornelius Scipio, the father of Scipio Africanus, consulted the Roman deputies at Marseilles about the cities of Gaul named Britannia, Narbonne, and Corbillo. Sanson identifies Britannia with the present town of Abbeville on the Somme. Dionysius, the author of "Perigesis," who wrote in the early part of the first century, mentions the Britanni as settled on the south of the Rhine, near the coast of Flanders.

Pliny, in his "Natural History," when recounting the various tribes on the coast of Gaul, mentions the Morini and Oramfaci as inhabiting the district of Boulogne, and places the Britanni between the last-named tribe and Amiens. (Pliny, lib. i., cap. xxxi.; Carte's "General History of England," vol i., p. 5).

"The Britanni on the Continent extended themselves farther along the coast than when first known to the Romans, and the branch of that tribe mentioned by Dionysius as settled on the coast of Flanders, and the Britons of Picardy mentioned by Pliny, were of the same nation and contiguous to each other. Dionysius further adds that they spread themselves farther south, even to the mouth of the Loire, and to the extremity of Armorica, which several writers say was called Britain long before it came into general use (Carte, p. 6).

"Sulpicius Severus, in his "Sacred Histories," gives an account of the Bishops summoned by the Emperor Constantius in the year 359 to the Council of Ariminium n Italy. Four hundred Bishops from Italy, Africa, Spain, and Gaul answered the summons, and the Emperor gave an order that all the Bishops were to be boarded and lodged, whilst the Council lasted, at the expense of the treasury. Whereupon Sulpicius, writing with pride of the action taken by the Bishops of the three provinces, Gallia, Aquitania, and Britannia, makes use of the following words: "Sed id nostris, id est. Aquitanis, Gallis, et Britannis, idecens visum; repudiatis fiscalibus propries sumptibus vivere maluerunt. Tres autem ex Britannia inopia proprii, publico usi sunt, cum oblatum a ceteris collationem respuissent; sanctius putantes, fescum gravare, quam singulos" (Lib. ji,, p. 401).

"The proposal seemed shameful to us, Aquitanians, Gauls, and Britons, who, rejecting the offer of help from the treasury, preferred to live at our own expense. Three, however, of the Bishops from Britannia, possessing no means of their own, refused to accept the maintenance offered by their brethren, deeming it a holier thing to burden the treasury than to accept aid from individuals" (Lib. ii., p. 401).

If any doubt exists as to the Britannia referred to, it is solved in the same book, p. 431. Sulpicius Severusi an Aquitanian by birth, speaks of the trial, condemnation and punishment of the Priscillian heretics by the secular Court at Treves in the year 389. Prisciallanus and his followers, Felicissimus, Armenianus, and a woman named Euchrosia were condemned to death and beheaded, but Instantias and Liberianus were banished to the Island of Sylena, "quas ultra Britanniarn sita est" (which is situated beyond Britain). Although it is not precisely known where the Island of Sylena was situated, except that it was somewhere beyond Britain, the Britain referred to surely must be Britain in Gaul, for it is incredible that the Gauls should possess a penal settlement in the North of Scotland, where Sylena must have been situated, if the words "beyond Britain" refer to the Island of Britain.

It is evident that if Sulpicius, who was born in 360—thirteen years before St. Patrick—could speak of Armorica as Britannia, and the Armorican Bishops as Britons, when he wrote his "Sacred Histories," it cannot be a matter of surprise that St. Patrick, if born in Armorica at a later period, should speak of himself as a Briton, and say that he had relatives among the Britons.

Armorica was called Britannia by Sulpicius Severus, but Sidonius Apollinarus, who flourished some time after, called the same country Armorica. It was not, however, unusual, as Carte points out, for the same people and the same country to be called by different names; for example, the Armorici and the Morini were one and the same people, whose names had the same signification—dwellers on the sea coast. (Carte, p. 16; Whitaker's "Genuine History of the Briton," pp. 216—219.)

As the historians just quoted are not concerned with the history of St. Patrick, but are simply tracing the origin and history of the Britons, their testimony is impartial.

Even Camden admits that Dionysius places the Britons on the maritime coast of Gaul, and renders his verses into English:—

> "Near the great pillars of the farthest land,
> The old Iberians, haughty souls, command
> Along the continent, where northern seas
> Roll their vast tides, and in cold billows rise:
> Where British nations in long tracts appear
> And fair-haired Germans ever famed in war."

The early existence of the Britons in Armorica did not depend on the settlement of the veteran Britons, who, having served under Constantino the Great, were rewarded by a gift of the vacant lands in Armorica, as William of Malmesbury narrates in his "History of the Kings"; or on the still larger settlement of Britons who fought for the usurper Maximus, which Ninius mentions, in the mysterious reference which embraced the whole country "from the Great St. Bernard in Piedmont to Cantavic in Picardy, and from Picardy to the western coast of France." The latter settlement took place between the years 383 and 388. The British refugees, who fled in terror from the Picts, Scots, and Saxons, may indeed have added to the numbers of Britons in Gaul from time immemorial, but they certainly were not the first to give the name Britannia to that country.

# BRITANNIAE IN THE PLURAL NOT APPROPRIATED TO GREAT BRITAIN

IT has been often urged, without any solid reason, that the plural Britannise used for Britain in the "Confession" can only refer to Great Britain, because that country was sub-divided by the Romans into five distinct provinces. The reason given cannot be convincing, because Catullus, who died in the year 54, used the plural for Britain before the Roman sub-divisions were made, when he wrote, "Nunc timent Galliae, timent Britanniae"—Caesar, "the Gauls and the Britons fear." The plural was used by St. Patrick when writing the "Confession" nearly one hundred years after the Romans with their divisions had left the country. It was used by Probus, who undoubtedly referred to Armoric Britain when writing about St. Patrick's native country, for he tells us in the plural that the Saint was born in Britain (natus in Britanniis). The plural was, therefore, used both for Britain in Gaul and for the Island of Britain.

The word Britannia occurs three times in the "Confession." In the "Book of Armagh" the name appears always in the plural, whilst in the Bollandist's copy of the "Confession" the name is printed once in the singular and twice in the plural. St. Jerome uses the singular always when referring to Britannia; and St. Bede, in his "History," uses the plural and singular indiscriminately. Whenever Britannia is mentioned, the context alone can guide us in distinguishing which Britain is meant. ("Ireland and St. Patrick," by the Rev. Bullen Morris, pp. 24, 25).

St. Patrick also mentions Gaul in the plural ("Gallias"), for although the whole country was subdivided into three separate nationalities—the Gauls, the Aquitanians, and the Britons—as Sulpicius Severus had already mentioned, the three provinces were called Gallise, or the Gauls, by the Romans. Galliae in the plural, therefore, either meant the whole country or any one of its sub-divisions, and the context alone could determine which province was meant.

Having these facts in mind, it is easy to interpret the words of St. Patrick: "Though I should have wished to leave them, and had been ready and very desirous of going to Britain [Britanniis], as if to my own country and parents; and not that alone, but to go even to Gaul (Gallias) to visit my brethren, and to see the face of the Lord's Saints, and God knows how ardently I wished it but I was bound in the Spirit, and He Who witnesseth will account me guilty if I do so—and I fear to lose the results of the labour which I have begun. And not I, but the Lord Jesus Christ, Who commanded me to come and remain with them for the rest of my life—if the Lord so will it, and keeps me from every evil way, that I should not sin before Him" ("Confession").

St. Patrick's relatives resided in the Gaulish province of Britain, and the disciples of St. Martin—"the Lord's Saints"—lived at Marmoutier in the province of Gaul. St. Patrick's natural desire was first to visit his relatives in Armorican Britain, and next to renew his friendship with the followers of St. Martin at Marmoutier, but God had decreed that he should spend all the rest of his days in the land of his adoption.

Gaul was not only the name of the whole country, which embraced three provinces—Gallia, Aquitania, and Britannia—it was also the name of one of the provinces. As Gaul in its widest sense was a different country from the Island of Britain, so the province of Gaul was quite distinct from the province of Armoric Britain. The Gauls, Aquitanians, and Britons, all possessing, as Csesar testifies, separate governments and different nationalities, regarded one another as distinct races. Thus Sulpicius Severus represents a Gaul as addressing some Aquitanians as follows: "When I think of myself as a Gaul about to address Aquitanians, I fear lest my uncultured speech should offend your too refined ears"—"Sed dum cogito me hominem Gallum inter Aquitanos verba facturum, vereor ne offendat nimium urbanas aures sermo rusticior" (Dialogue 20).

# ST. PATRICK CALLS COROTICUS, A BRITISH PRINCE, "FELLOW CITIZEN"

IT is objected again that St. Patrick called the followers of Coroticus, who were Britons, his fellow citizens, and that, therefore, the Saint and the island Britons are of the same nationality.

The objection is founded on St. Patrick's "Epistle to Coroticus," in which the following words occur: "I have vowed to my God to teach this people, although I should be despised by them, to whom I have written with my own hand to be given to the soldiers to be forwarded to Coroticus. I do not say to my fellow citizens, nor to the fellow citizens of the pious Romans, but to the fellow citizens of the devil, through their evil deeds and hostile practices."

As the Romans had abandoned Britain long before the letter to Coroticus was written, it is somewhat difficult to understand the precise meaning of the words just quoted: "I do not say to my fellow citizens, or to the fellow citizens of the pious Romans," unless some of the soldiers of Coroticus were, like St. Patrick, Roman freemen. The word "citizen" in the Roman sense was as wide as the extent of the Roman Empire.

Although the soldiers of Coroticus are also called "fellow citizens of the pious Romans," no one would surely dream of saying that the soldiers of Coroticus and the pious Roman were actually of the same nationality. St. Patrick could, therefore, call the soldiers of Coroticus in the same sense his "fellow citizens," without implying that he was of the same race. If, however, the soldiers of Coroticus were Roman freemen, they would be fellow citizens of St. Patrick and fellow citizens of the Romans, although of different nationalities. The indignant protest made by the Saint in the same letter, that "free-born Christian men are sold and enslaved amongst the wicked, abandoned, and apostate Picts," greatly favours our interpretation of "fellow citizens."

It must, however, be acknowledged that there is a considerable amount of obscurity about the meaning of the words, which are so confidently interpreted as signifying that the Apostle of Ireland was a native of Great Britain. But the words as they stand cannot be fairly assumed to prove that St. Patrick was a "fellow countryman" of the soldiers of Coroticus, unless they prove with equal force that the Romans were of the same nationality as the soldiers of Coroticus. The quotation proves too much and, therefore, it proves nothing.

# SUMMARY

HAVING given the different theories concerning the native country of St. Patrick, and having faithfully quoted all that the Seven old Latin "Lives" of the Saint have narrated on this subject, and given our reasons for accepting the Armoric theory as the most reasonable solution of the problem, it will be advisable to give a brief summary of the arguments brought forward to prove that St. Patrick was an Armorican Britain, born at Boulogne-sur-Mer.

Boulogne-sur-Mer, or ancient Bononia, was called by the same name, "Bonaven," as the town in which St. Patrick implies that he was born. Boulogne possessed a Roman encampment, and it was, therefore, Bonaven Taberniae, mentioned in the "Confession."

Caligula's tower, on the north-eastern cliffs, in the town and within the suburbs, was called "Turris Ordinis" by the Romans, but "Nemtor" by the Gaulish Celts, as Hersart de la Villemarque states in his "Celtic Legend."

It is certain that Niall of the Nine Hostages made use of the Port of Boulogne when he invaded Armorica in the twenty-seventh year of his reign, and that he died at that port after his assassination.

It is probable that Niall sailed to Boulogne when invading Armorica on the first occasion, for he was carrying his arms into the same country, of which Boulogne was the principal port, and the only one used by the Romans when invading England.

The return "of Niall" from his first expedition into-Armorica with captives, including St. Patrick, on board in the year 388, corresponds precisely with the fifteenth year of St. Patrick, who was born in the year 373. This fact is not only testified by Keating, but by Hersart de la Villemarque in his "Celtic Legend," who narrates that Calphurnius, St. Patrick's father, was a Roman officer in charge of Nemtor, near which his family resided in a Roman villa, and that Calphurnius was slain, and St. Patrick made captive by a hostile fleet that came from Ireland.

As Nemtor was not only the name of the tower, but the district of the tower, and situated within the suburbs of Bonaven, St. Fiacc's account of his patron's birthplace, which simply gives the name of the district, and St. Patrick's statement that his home was in the suburban district of Bonaven, harmonise together.

The Scholiast and the author of the Trepartite "Life," by admitting that the Saint was captured in Armorica, annul their assertion that he was born in Scotland, because St. Patrick distinctly states that his family hailed from Bonaven Tabernise, or Boulogne, and that he was captured while residing at his father's villula. The

Scholiast and Tripartite "Life" consequently admit that Bonaven Taberniae was situated in Armorica.

The impression that Bononia, or Boulogne, was St. Patrick's native town is confirmed by Probus; he narrates all the misfortune that overtook Calphurnius and his family whilst they were quietly living in their own native country (in patria), and in their own seaside city in Armorica.

Armorica was then included in the Province of Neustria, one of the sub-divided kingdoms of the Franks, and it was on that account that Probus states that St. Patrick was born in Neustria.

Ware, Usher, and Cardinal Moran, who cling to the Scotch theory of St. Patrick's birth, all contradict the Scholiast, who asserts that St. Patrick was born in Dumbarton; whilst those who hold fast to the Dumbarton theory make frantic efforts to convert the Crag into a heavenly tower.

St. Patrick, after the vision, in which he was told that he should return to his own native country, sailed to Gaul and not to the Island of Britain.

It had been proved on the authority of Sulpicius Severus, who was born in the year 360, that Armorica was called Britannia, and the Armoricans were called Britons when the Council of Ariminium was held in the year 359—fourteen years before the birth of St. Patrick. The Saint, when writing his "Confession" in 493, when the province had even a stronger claim to the name, could emphatically say, if he was born in Armorica, that he was a Briton and had relatives amongst the Britons.

# THE SITE OF THE VILLULA
# WHERE ST. PATRICK WAS BORN

FRENCH archeologists point out the "Hotel du Pavillion et des Bains de Mer," facing the sea-bathing place at Boulogne, as occupying the site from which Caligula's tower, Nemthur, once lifted its head into the heavens and shed its light over land and sea. On the frowning cliff which casts its shadow over the hotel there is a mass of hard brick ruins—the last remnants of the fortifications built round Nemtor when Boulogne was captured by the British troops in 1544.

Calphurnius's villula was evidently situated somewhere on the plateau, called Tour d'Ordre, between the tower and the town, for St. Patrick, in his "Confession," assured us that his father's home was near to ("prope") Bonaven, a statement which he would not make if the villula stood on the sea-coast beyond the tower. It is, therefore, certain that the site of the villula still exists somewhere not far inland from the ruins alluded to.

Although Nemtor was undermined by the sea and fell into the waves in 1649, a picture of the tower as it once stood in all its glory is still to be seen in the museum of Boulogne, and the curator very kindly permitted the writer of this little history to get the drawing copied, so that the sons of St. Patrick might be permitted to view Nemtor, which Calphurnius lost his life in defending, and which gave a name to the district in which St. Patrick was born.

If this brief history of St. Patrick's native town has succeeded in identifying ancient Bononia, now Boulogne-sur-Mer, as St. Patrick's birthplace, then the whole plateau of Tour d'Ordre, on the north-eastern cliffs of Boulogne, where the villula of Calphurnius once stood, will become sacred in the eyes of the spiritual sons of St. Patrick throughout the wide world.

**THE PRESENT FORTIFICATIONS AND SITE OF THE ROMAN
ENCAMPMENT AT BOULOGNE.**

Lector House believes that a society develops through a two-fold approach of continuous learning and adaptation, which is derived from the study of classic literary works spread across the historic timeline of literature records. Therefore, we aim at reviving, repairing and redeveloping all those inaccessible or damaged but historically as well as culturally important literature across subjects so that the future generations may have an opportunity to study and learn from past works to embark upon a journey of creating a better future.

This book is a result of an effort made by Lector House towards making a contribution to the preservation and repair of original ancient works which might hold historical significance to the approach of continuous learning across subjects.

HAPPY READING & LEARNING!

LECTOR HOUSE LLP
E-MAIL: lectorpublishing@gmail.com